SINGAPORE

by Evelyn Sebastian

with photographs by
Jacky Yip, Magnus Bartlett,
Alain Evrard and Cameraman Ltd

HUNTER
PUBLISHING INC

Published by CFW Publications Ltd
1602 Alliance Building
130 Connaught Road Central
Hong Kong

U.S. edition published 1988 by
Hunter Publishing, Inc.,
Edison, NJ 08818

Printed in Hong Kong

Acknowledgements
I wish to express my grateful thanks and appreciation to Cheong Swee-keng of the Singapore Tourist Promotion Board in Hong Kong and Rosey Wong for their invaluable assistance in the gathering and checking of information contained in this book. Thanks are also due to P. Nirmala and Christina Ng Sue Chin of STPB in Singapore, Pauline Yu and Mary Anne Lim of Singapore Airlines, and all those who, in one way or another, helped in the book's production.

Other titles available in the POST GUIDE series:
Australia
Hong Kong
Japan
Malaysia
Indonesia
Sri Lanka
Thailand
The Philippines

ISBN 1-55650-159-5

Glow-worms of light from the buildings on Shenton Way.

Contents

Introduction

Singapore is one of the most progressive countries in Asia. It has emerged from the ranks of the developing countries to become an economic leader, held up as an example of a success story.

Many who grew up picturing Singapore as it was in the days of Somerset Maugham still invest it with a lifestyle that belongs to another era, epitomized by the Raffles Hotel, that grand old dowager of hotels in whose gracious grounds many an elegant social event took place. They imagine old colonial bungalows with wide cooking verandas set amidst lush tropical gardens and a tempo of life that is slow and easy. Imbued with immortality by the retelling of stories and nurtured by memories, these images linger on until a new set replaces them.

A visit to Singapore today will instantly dispel those images. Only a few colonial-style buildings remain. One can still see two-story brick-roofed buildings painted in pastel shades of blue, pink, yellow and green and embellished like Wedgwood jasper ware, but few are in a state of preservation. Most are crumbling, their days numbered.

The enclaves of the Chinese, Indian and Arab merchants set up in the early and mid-19th century still exist, full of character and life, but the threat of encroaching merchandising hangs heavily over them.

The beehive of activity that once surrounded the Singapore River has died down, and the old warehouses lie abandoned, like ghost towns. There is still water traffic, barges bringing in their assorted cargo, but the river is no longer the lifeblood of commerce as it used to be during the days of Sir Stamford Raffles. The face of Singapore has changed greatly in the past twenty years. Centers of commerce are shifting. Smart new places are opening up; new towns burgeoning. Everywhere one sees the thrust of skyscrapers and towering office blocks, multi-story housing estates with their own complex of playgrounds, schools, temples, churches and markets.

In various parts of the island republic massive construction projects are in progress. Cranes are poised over development sites; there are gaping holes where old buildings have been torn down by the wrecker's ball, preparatory to redevelopment. In some places that were once virgin forests or fallow field, bulldozers are at work churning up red earth to make way for new towns. Reclamation work goes on steadily, wresting land from the sea. At the rate changes are taking place, Singapore will look completely different from what it was in 1900, except for a few churches, temples, houses and other buildings that have been declared national monuments by the government.

Marina City and Raffles City. Completed sometime in the mid-1980s, Marina City and Raffles City add a new dimension to Singapore entertainment and recreational facilities.

Barges tied up along the Singapore River.

Marina City, envisioned as an extension of the East Coast development, took shape on a land mass, which only a few years ago, was nothing but the sea. Reclamation work carried out at the confluence of the Singapore River and the Straits of Malacca has produced several hectares of valuable property. The complex is dominated by three high-rise hotels: the 591-room Singapore Oriental is operated by Mandarin International Hotels; the 613-room Marina Mandarin is managed by Mandarin Singapore International Hotels Pte Ltd, and the 845-room Pan Pacific Singapore which is under the management of Tokyu Hotels International of Japan. The 30-story Pan Pacific is a convention hotel and exhibition area and is topped by a revolving restaurant with a panoramic view of the surrounding.

An integral part of the complex are the shops and shopping mall on a podium shaped like a cross and featuring landscaped gardens with fountains and waterfalls, a swimming pool and squash courts. At each corner of the four corners of the complex is a department store.

The **Raffles City** project is built on prime land that was occupied for 159 years by the Raffles Institution, a school founded by Raffles himself. The city-within-a-city encompasses two hotels managed by Westin Hotel Company, an office tower block, a convention area, shops, restaurants, recreational facilities and a car park. The complex also boast the tallest hotel building in the world – the 71-story, 1200-room Raffles City Hotel. The companion hotel has a 28-story twin-core tower with 800 guest rooms. Between the two hotels, guests and patrons have a selection of 15 food and beverage outlets, not to mention the other restaurants within the complex. The hotels have a swimming pool, gymnasium and health club, tennis and squash courts. The convention center – the largest in Singapore – is housed in the podium, the main feature of which is a seven-story atrium with a skylight.

The construction and upgrading of existing roads and thoroughfares continues. Ribbon-smooth expressways link the island from end to end, cutting down traveling time. But with increasing affluence, more vehicular traffic clogs the roads and railways.

The long-term solution to this problem is the Mass Rapid Transit System (MRT). The feasibility of the system sparked much controversy but the government gave the green light for its construction. The S$5 billion, 70-km (43.5-miles) long urban railway system opened in 1988 with the North Line from Yi Shun and Marina Bay and the West Line from Jurong to City Hall. The East Line from Changi to Central is due to open in 1990.

One thing remains: the tropical character of Singapore. By meticulous planning and foresight, Singapore is never permitted to be other than what it claims to be: the Garden City of Asia. Masses of greenery everywhere give it a refreshingly clean look, and venerable old trees still spread their leafy branches over wide boulevards and small

side streets. Clusters of flowering shrubs flaunt their brilliance
everywhere. The frequent tropical rains dispel the dust that can coat
plants and trees a drab brown, and give them a newly washed, dewy
look.

There are still remnants of the old colorful Singapore. Strolling
about Chinatown, Arab Street and Serangoon Road (dubbed Little
India) with their distinct sights, sounds and smells gives one an idea of
the ethnic character of Singapore, where people live out their lives much
as they did in the past when these communities were self-contained and
racial distinctions were sharper, more delineated.

Batik sellers and carpet merchants proliferate in the shadow of the
mosque around the area of Arab Street where, on the nights of Ramadan,
all types of Malay delicacies are sold. Serangoon Road offers sumptuous
silk sarees and the exotic spices of the East much sought after by the
empires of the West in the long-ago days. In Chinatown, small shops
bulging with merchandise line alleyways. Market stalls mushroom in
the middle of streets while people, stray animals, bicycles and trishaws
try to squeeze in between. But sections of Chinatown are in danger of
being swallowed in the maw of the bulldozer. Rows of old shops are
being demolished. Their torn interiors, littered with a fragment of a
showcase here, glass shards there, and old boxes and mutilated objects
everywhere, tell the tale that progress is encroaching.

Instant Asia was once the advertising catchphrase for Singapore. If
you sit in the lobby of one of the luxury hotels in town or at any of the
city's nightclubs, you will see (while sipping your Singapore Gin Sling) a
parade of races: Chinese, Malays, Indians, Europeans, Arabs and
Eurasians. They make up the polyglot population of Singapore. This
multiracial, multi-language and multi-religious melange is what gives
Singapore its distinct character.

Singaporeans from various walks of life are proud of their ethnic
background and while they nurture their cultural differences (as evidenced
by their food, religious beliefs, customs and festivals) they think of
themselves as Singaporeans first. Intent on improving their standard of
living, they lay great stress on education, family planning, and technology.
Some areas of their life may be restricted, but they can't complain. They are
not economically deprived. And, to them, that's what counts.

History

Long before the first wave of Portuguese explorers in search of the
fabled spice islands reached the eastern shore, Singapore was already in
existence. Chinese explorers of the 3rd century knew it then as
Poluochung, probably a transliteration of the Malay words Pulau Ujong,
meaning "island at the end of Peninsula". Arab, Indian and Malay
traders knew it as Tumasek (variously spelled Temasek and Tumasik),
meaning "Sea Town" in Malay.

(above) Moslems at preyer. (opposite page) A typical Malay wedding.

It was a prince from the Sri Vijayan empire – Sri Tri Buana – who gave the island of Singapore its name. According to legend, this prince left the empire of Palembang in Sumatra in the 12th century in search of a kingdom. He arrived on the island of Tumasek on the Strait of Johor and while exploring the island, the prince reportedly saw an animal which he thought was a lion. Thereupon he called the island **Singa Pura** – "Lion City" in Sanskrit.

It is not certain whether the prince saw a lion or not. But the name Singapore (from Singa Pura) endures. Today the symbol of Singapore is the Merlion, half lion and half fish. Its eight-meter (26-ft) high statue stands guard over the mouth of the Singapore River and can be seen by ships out on the harbor.

The island's fortunes rose and fell with the rise and fall of the rival kingdoms of Java, Sumatra and Siam who fought for control of the Malay states. When the Sri Vijayan empire declined in the 13th century, the Javanese Majapahit empire took over. Several wars were waged on the shores of Singa Pura but the invaders were repeatedly repulsed, until a traitor among the defenders revealed to the invaders the entrance to the island. So fierce was the ensuing battle that the island was devastated. But life continued for the survivors and the victors. Tumasek flourished as a fishing village and soon it became an important base for the Majapahits in their command of the seas.

The Siamese eventually displaced the Majapahits, putting the island under the rule of Tamagi. This worthy was murdered by a renegade Majapahit prince, Parameswara, who, having succeeded to power, began to indulge in acts of piracy. Thus Singa Pura became the base for marauders of the seas who preyed upon the cargo ships laden with their treasures. Parameswara in turn was deposed by the invading Siamese army who destroyed a powerful princedom of the Malay Buddhists until, in the 19th century, an official of the British East India Company – Sir Thomas Stamford Raffles – arrived on the island and changed the course of its history.

Four centuries earlier, the Portuguese had discovered the route to the East and the spice trade, and had planted the cross and the flag in various parts of the eastern seas. The Dutch followed in their wake, then the British. Britain's interest in Southeast Asia grew as her trade with China expanded. By the end of the 18th century, Britain was in control of the lucrative tea trade between China and Europe. It soon became apparent to the British that they had to establish an independent settlement that was strategically located to serve both as a naval base and a port of call for British shipping between India and China. Penang was acquired, and for a time it operated as a free port. But it was not the success the British had expected it to be. For one thing it proved to be a financial burden; for another, the location was not favorable for the China trade.

In 1805, Thomas Stamford Raffles, who worked as a clerk for ten years in London with the East India Company, arrived in Penang to assume the post of assistant secretary to the Governor. He was accompanied by his new bride, Olivia Fancourt, an attractive widow ten years his senior, and his father, mother and sister. During the long sea voyage, he started to learn Malay tongue. His interest in the language and culture deepened while in Penang and he became an expert in Malay affairs.

A man of ambition and far-sighted vision, he began to think of a trading base that would establish Britain's supremacy in her trade with the East. He made his views known to the then Governor-General of India Lord Minto, who had jurisdiction over Penang and Malacca. Lord Minto shared Raffles' views; he was, in fact, considering the capture of Java from the Dutch. Consequently he summoned Raffles to a meeting in Calcutta and thereafter appointed Raffles his Agent in the Malay states, with Malacca as his base. From there he was to prepare for the invasion. This posting provided Raffles with valuable information about the region and when the campaign against Java proved successful, Lord Minto named him Lieutenant-Governor of Java. He was a good administrator, introducing many liberal reforms of far-reaching consequence.

About this time the protracted war between Britain and France was settled, and under the London Convention signed in 1814, Britain agreed to return to Holland all the Dutch possessions she held in the archipelago. In 1816 Raffles sailed back to England, alone. His wife, Olivia, had died earlier. While in England he published his book, **The History of Java**, which met with success. He was knighted in 1817 and the East India Company named him Lieutenant Governor of Bencoolen, a British outpost in Sumatra. Raffles married again, and in winter of 1817 set sail again once more for the East.

His dream of a British empire in the East was as strong as ever, and he continued to communicate with the Governor-General in Calcutta (Lord Hastings). Finally he was given permission to search for a suitable base to replace Penang. His search brought him to the shores of Singapore on 28 January 1819.

When Raffles landed in Singapore, he liked what he saw: a fine natural harbor with a sheltered anchorage, and a strategic location that made it an ideal base for trade. In a letter addressed to a friend in England, Raffles described Singapore as "the naval of the Malay countries", foreseeing it as a port that must "eventually destroy the spell of Dutch monopoly."

Less than a month after his landing, he had obtained a concession from the nominal rulers of Singapore – the Temenggong and Sultan Hussein – to establish a trading post on the coast between Tanjong Malang and the Kallang River. Another treaty signed in June 1823 granted the East India Company full control to trade in Singapore. The island was finally ceded in perpetuity to the company in 1824 in exchange for cash payments and larger pensions for the Temenggong and Sultan Hussein.

Until that time, Singapore had been governed as a residency under Bencoolen, headed by Sir Stamford Raffles. It was Raffles who laid the groundwork for modern-day Singapore. After the cession, Singapore was placed directly under the control of the Governor-General and Council of the East India Company in India.

British influence was established on the periphery of the Malay peninsula with the incorporation in 1826 of Singapore, Penang and Malacca (acquired from the Dutch in 1795) into the Straits Settlements. But this influence extended only to trade and it was not until the 1870s that Britain played an active political role in the region. For the first few years the Straits Settlements were under the supervision of Penang. In 1831, they were placed under the government in Bengal. This was changed again in 1851 when the Governor-General took personal supervision of the settlements. After the Indian Mutiny in 1857-9, the governing of India passed from the hands of the East India Company to the India Office in London, and the administration of the Straits Settlements was finally transferred to the civil authorities. In 1867, Singapore was made a British colony.

Singapore grew rapidly from the time it was founded by Raffles. Its status as a free port drew many merchants to its shores and trade expanded, especially after the opening of the Suez Canal in 1869.

(overleaf) These buildings reflect Singapore's colonial past.

VICTORIA MEMORIAL HALL

As they grew more affluent, the influential merchant class started to clamor for participation in government affairs. This was brought to an abrupt end by the Japanese invasion and occupation in World War II, from 15 February 1942 to 5 September 1945. The voices were heard again after the war, when Singapore became a separate crown colony after Penang and Malacca joined the Malayan Union in 1946, marking the dissolution of the Straits Settlements. In the first election for Legislative Council in 1948, nine out of 22 seats were won by locals. A new constitution was introduced in 1955 providing for a Legislative Assembly with an elected majority of 25 out of a total of 32 members.

A constitutional conference held in London in 1957 agreed in principle to give Singapore internal self-government. In a general election for the first fully-elected Legislative Assembly on 30 May 1959, the People's Action Party emerged victorious, winning 43 seats out of 51. Singapore at last achieved internal self-government on 3 June 1959. For a brief while, it was an independent state within the Federation of Malaysia until it attained its status as an independent and sovereign state on 9 August 1965. Singapore was the 117th nation to be admitted as a member of the United Nations and the 22nd member of the British Commonwealth of Nations. Under a constitutional amendment passed on 22 December 1965, the State of Singapore became the Republic of Singapore.

Government

Singapore has a parliamentary form of government with a unicameral assembly consisting of 75 members elected by secret ballot in single member constituencies. The Parliament elects a President for a term of four years and the President in turn appoints one member of Parliament who commands the confidence of the majority of its members as Prime Minister. Under the Prime Minister a cabinet consisting of 14 ministers who are appointed by the President on the advice of the Prime Minister.

The present ruling party, in continuous power since 1959 (having won six consecutive elections), is the People's Action Party. At the helm is the dynamic, aggressive, Cambridge-educated Mr Lee Kuan Yew, Prime Minister of Singapore. From the early years of Singapore's statehood through its struggle for independence and up to the present time, the leadership has rested on his shoulders. Some people may consider him a benevolent dictator, but there is no doubt that much of what Singapore is today was shaped by him and his party.

Economy

The worldwide economic recession has affected Singapore's growth rate but the island republic has learned to cope with the bad times and under Mr Lee is prepared to remedy the economic ills by hard work and by upgrading its industrial technology.

The island's unique geographical location along one of the most important shipping lanes in the world makes it an ideal conduit for the flow of goods, especially rubber, tin and spices from neighboring countries, and manufactured goods from overseas. More than 300 shipping lines use its port facilities. Its harbor is the second busiest in the world, next only to Rotterdam. Vessels enter and leave the port at the rate of one every fifteen minutes.

Singapore engages in tin smelting, oil refining, rubber and copra processing and light industry. It is one of the largest oil refining, blending and distributing centers in the world and is a major supplier of electronic components. Its major income-earners are the manufacturing sector (22%), trade and industry (20%), banking and finance (18%). Textiles and electronics lead the manufactured goods.

The government encourages investment proposals which introduced skill-intensive manufacturing and service activities, particularly those producing or serving electrical and electronics products, machinery and precision engineering, transport equipment and heavy, basic metal engineering, petroleum, chemicals and petrochemicals.

To meet the needs of industry, Singapore is engaged in the development of its manpower resources. Technical skills are increasingly emphasized in the schools, for instance, it is compulsory for all boys in secondary schools to learn technical subjects such as workshop practice and blueprint reading, regardless of the careers they will finally choose. The training of skilled and semiskilled workers falls on the Vocational Industrial Training Board (VITB) and the Economic Development Board (EDB).

Population

There are more than 2.58 million Singaporeans (78 per cent native-born) according to 1982 statistics, compared to 10,683 reported when the first census took place in 1824, and the 120 Malays and 20 Chinese counted when Sir Thomas Stamford Raffles landed in the fishing village in 1819. Chinese* predominate, constituting 76.9 per cent of the population. The Malays are a far second, with 14.6 per cent; the Indians, classed together with the Pakistanis, Bangladeshis and Sri Lankans, form 6.4 per cent, and other ethnic groups account for 2.1 per cent.

*There is a sub-group among the Chinese, almost regarded as a different race, referred to as the 'Peranakans' (males are called babas and females nonyas, perhaps a corruption of the Portuguese term for lady). The Peranakans are Straits-born Chinese, the descendants of the Han Chinese who settled in the Malay peninsula in the 14th century and blended their own Chinese language and culture (mainly Hokkien, Teochew and Hakka) with that of the Malays. Associated with the Peranakans was wealth and social standing. They belonged to the ruling class and during the colonial days were civil servants and overlords of the Dutch, Portuguese and English. There is a distinct Peranakan cuisine (see FOOD AND DRINK, p.72), style of dress and home decoration. One of the most distinguished nonyas in Singapore is Mrs Lee Chin Koon, the mother of the Prime Minister.

(above) Traffic congestion: a city problem.
(opposite page) Malacca-style houses on Cuppage Road.

The government's campaign for a two-child family is aimed at achieving a zero population growth by the year 2030. When this scheme was first announced in 1965 it was met with widespread protest, but the government has put more teeth into the campaign by making it tough for those who insist on having more than two children. Incentives are tax concessions for the first three children; maternity leave for civil servants and employees in private enterprise for the first two children (delivery charges in government hospitals are increased after the first childbirth), and giving preference to a two-child family in the selection of primary schools. Those who have have three or more will just have to take what's left after the privileged families have made their choice.

Newspapers, posters, radio and television and cinema carry advertisements in Chinese, English, Malay and Tamil advocating family planning. More than 50 clinics offer free advice on birth control, and contraceptives are dispensed at nominal prices. Abortions are available during the first four months of pregnancy. Fifth- and sixth-graders are taught the importance of small families.

At the Science Centre, the Life Sciences gallery attracts a large number of visitors. Schoolchildren flock to view the exhibits and lighted displays in genetics, evolution, population, human birth and ecology sections. Films are regularly shown at the family planning theatre and population theatre. Schoolgirls silently watch a film of an actual childbirth on a small video screen, while nearby, younger children observe intently as chicks peck their way out of their shells. The section on demography relates population with food supply and warns against the dangers of overpopulation.

Priority in getting public housing is also given to two-child families. As more than 68 per cent of the population live in apartments provided by the government, this is an important consideration.

Housing

Before 1960, a large segment of Singapore's population lived in sub-standard housing. Today the majority live in low-cost accommodation with full amenities and the number of those owning their homes is growing. The responsibility for public housing falls on two government agencies: the Housing Development Board which caters for the middle- and lower-income groups and the Housing and Urban Development Corporation, mainly responsible for providing housing for middle- to upper middle-income groups. Then there are the private town houses, apartments, condominiums and bungalows. There is usually a long waiting list for those dwellings – and most are for sale, not for rent. At the lower end of the market, HDB apartments cost at least S$80,000 a unit (three bedrooms, a kitchen, dining and living area); HUDC units as much as S$250,000, while private houses can go as high as S$1.5 million.

When the government launched its building program in 1960, it concentrated on providing low-cost housing for slum dwellers; then in the mid-60s it encouraged Singaporeans to buy their own homes under the Home Ownership Scheme. In the 70s construction was stepped up, and 243,396 housing units were completed, despite the recession, shortage of workers and escalating building costs. The government is now into its sixth Five-Year Building Program, and its emphasis is on quality living. The new housing units in the new towns have larger floor areas, better fittings and a more congenial atmosphere. Older housing estates are being upgraded to improve their living environment.

Financing comes mainly from the Central Provident Fund, a compulsory national insurance savings scheme.

Language

Malay, Chinese (Mandarin), Tamil and English are the four official languages; Malay is the national language while English remains the language of administration and commerce. Hokkien, Teochew (known as Chiu Chow in other countries), Cantonese, Hainanese, Hakka and Foochow are the main Chinese dialects but Mandarin is increasingly being used instead of the dialects. The ethnics Indians speak Telegu, Malayalam, Punjabi, Hindi and Bengali.

Religion

The religious freedom and harmony on this island republic is reflected in the shining domes and minarets of mosques, the soaring steeple sand slender spires of churches, the ornamented roofs and ornate facades of temples that punctuate the city's skyline. The main religions are Buddhism, Christianity, Hinduism, Islam and Taoism. Other religious groupings include Jains, Jews, Sikhs and Zoroastrians.

The temples, churches and mosques of Singapore are of architectural and historic interest and are among the national monuments of the island republic (see pp.96-100).

General Information

Climate

Lying on the tropical zone, approximately 136.8 km (85 miles) north of the equator, Singapore has a hot and humid climate, but cooling sea breezes make the heat bearable. Daytime temperatures average about 30.6°C (87°F), dropping in the evenings to a pleasant 23.5°C (74°F). Singapore is regularly refreshed by rains. These are likely to be sudden but brief downpours, giving the island a clean, newly-washed look. The heaviest rainfall occurs between November and January, during the northeast monsoon season, and the least rainfall in July, during the southwest monsoon. In between the monsoon months are thunderstorms known as *sumatras*, occurring mostly in the morning and between April and May and October and November. The coolest months are from November to January, with February as the sunniest month.

What to pack: Lightweight clothes in natural fibers and comfortable shoes and sandals are the best. Dress is generally casual. Most places accept short-sleeved, open-necked shirts for men. In some places and on certain occasions a jacket and tie may be *de rigueur*, but informality is more often the rule than the exception. When in doubt as to the correct dress, call the restaurant in question, or enquire from your host. There are many shops selling kaftans and printed summer wear, in case women feel they have to augment their wardrobe.

Entry and Exit Formalities

A valid passport or an internationally recognized travel document is required for entry to Singapore. You don't need a visa if you are a citizen of:
* The United Kingdom, Commonwealth countries, the Republic of Ireland;
* Liechtenstein, Monaco, the Netherlands, San Marino and Switzerland;
* The United States (unless you are going to Singapore for employment or for residence);

CITY OF SINGAPORE
KIM TIAN RD.
TIONG BAHRU RD.
P
LIM LIAK ST.
SENG POH RD.
ENG HOON ST.
JALAN BUKIT MERAH
SPOONER RD.
COLLEGE RD.
HOSPITAL DR.
KG. BAHRU RD.
OUTRAM RD.
OUTRAM PARK
Iseta
Em
CHIN SWEE RD.
KEPPEL RD.
SPOTTISWOODE PARK RD.
Station
EU TONG SEN ST.
NEIL RD.
KEONG SAIK RD.
PARK CRESCENT
People's
Park
Kreta Ayer
People's
Theatre
P
PAGAR RD.
ENGGOR ST.
SMITH ST.
TEMPLE ST.
PAGODA ST.
NEW
BRIDGE
RD.
UPPER CROSS ST.
SOUTH BRIDGE RD.
P
NORTH CANAL RD.
ANSON RD.
WALLICH ST.
MAXWELL RD.
P
Thian
Hock
Keng
Temple
TELOK AYER ST.
AMOY ST.
CLUB ST.
CROSS ST.
PEKIN ST.
CHURCH ST.
SOUTH CANAL
PRINCE EDWARD RD.
Singapore
Conference
Hall
P
SHENTON WAY
ROBINSON RD.
BOAT
QUAY
Singapore Rive
RAFFLES QUAY
COLLYER QUAY
BATTERY RD.
FULLERTON
RD.
G.P.O.
Me
P
Clifford
Pier
Hotel
Place of Interest
P Post Office
yiu

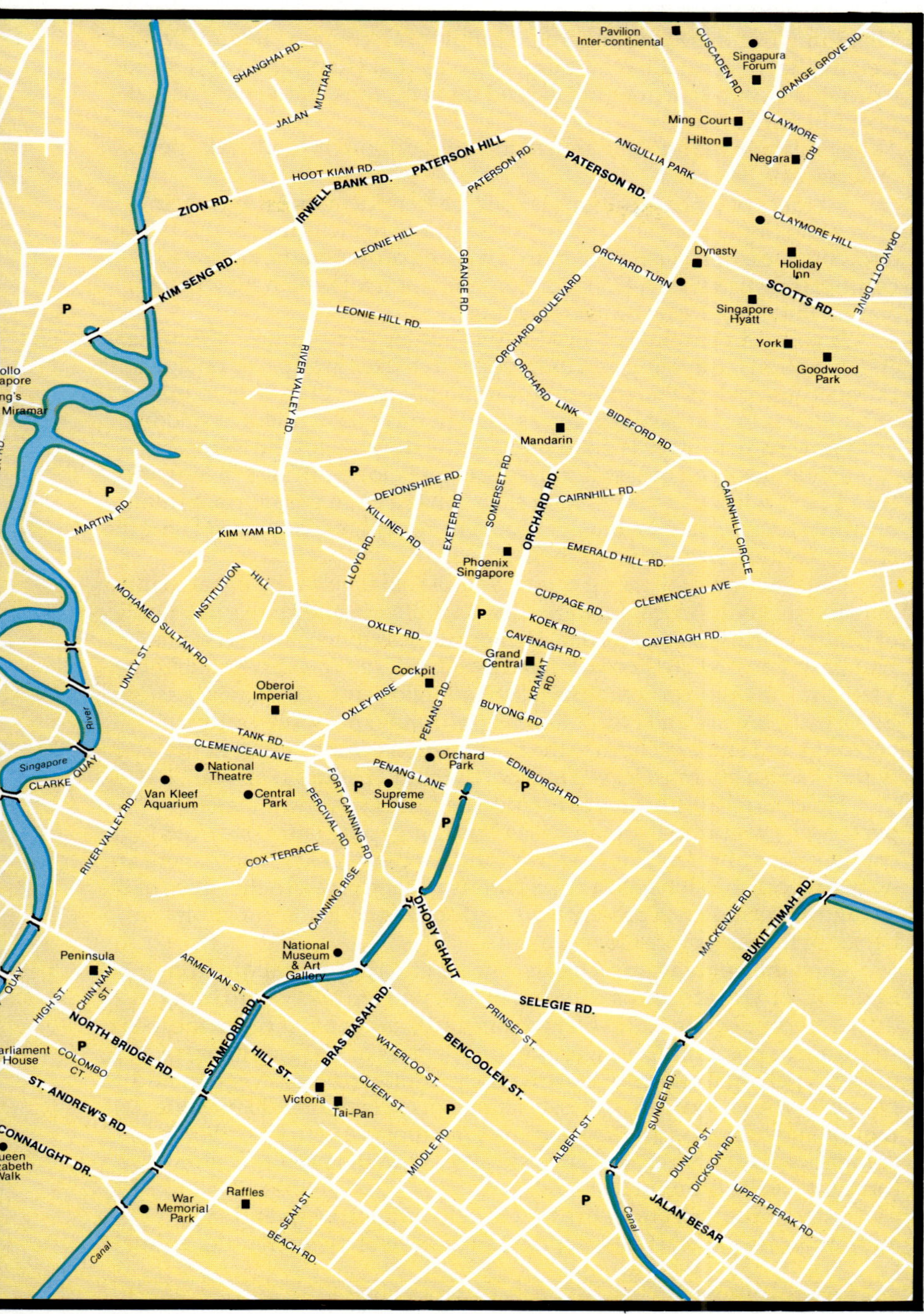

Pavilion
Inter-continental
CUSCADEN RD.
Singapura
Forum
ORANGE GROVE RD.
Ming Court
Hilton
CLAYMORE RD.
Negara
Angullia Park
SHANGHAI RD.
JALAN MUTIARA
CLAYMORE HILL
HOOT KIAM RD.
PATERSON HILL
IRWELL BANK RD.
PATERSON RD.
PATERSON RD.
ZION RD.
Paterson Rd.
DRAYCOTT DRIVE
LEONIE HILL
Dynasty
Orchard Turn
Holiday Inn
KIM SENG RD.
GRANGE RD.
SCOTTS RD.
LEONIE HILL RD.
Orchard Boulevard
Singapore Hyatt
P
York
Goodwood Park
RIVER VALLEY RD.
Apollo
Singapore
King's
Miramar
Orchard Link
BIDEFORD RD.
P
Mandarin
DEVONSHIRE RD.
Somerset RD.
P
MARTIN RD.
CAIRNHILL RD.
MARTIN RD.
KIM YAM RD.
EXETER RD.
ORCHARD RD.
CAIRNHILL CIRCLE
KILLINEY RD.
Emerald Hill RD.
INSTITUTION HILL
LLOYD RD.
Phoenix Singapore
MOHAMED SULTAN RD.
OXLEY RD.
CUPPAGE RD.
CLEMENCEAU AVE.
UNITY ST.
P
KOEK RD.
CAVENAGH RD.
Cockpit
CAVENAGH RD.
Oberoi Imperial
Grand Central
KRAMAT RD.
River
OXLEY RISE
PENANG RD.
BUYONG RD.
TANK RD.
CLEMENCEAU AVE.
Singapore
Orchard Park
EDINBURGH RD.
QUAY
National Theatre
Penang Lane
P
CLARKE
Van Kleef Aquarium
Central Park
Supreme House
P
RIVER VALLEY RD.
FORT CANNING RD.
PERCIVAL RD.
COX TERRACE
CANNING RISE
MACKENZIE RD.
BUKIT TIMAH RD.
DHOBY GHAUT
Peninsula
ARMENIAN ST.
National Museum & Art Gallery
SELEGIE RD.
SUNGEI RD.
QUAY
CHIN NAM ST.
STAMFORD RD.
BRAS BASAH RD.
PRINSEP ST.
HIGH ST.
NORTH BRIDGE RD.
WATERLOO ST.
BENCOOLEN ST.
Parliament House
P
COLOMBO CT.
HILL ST.
QUEEN ST.
DUNLOP ST.
ST. ANDREW'S RD.
Victoria
Tai-Pan
P
ALBERT ST.
DICKSON RD.
CONNAUGHT DR.
MIDDLE RD.
UPPER PERAK RD.
Queen Elizabeth Walk
P
Raffles
SEAH ST.
JALAN BESAR
War Memorial Park
Canal
BEACH RD.
Canal

* Belgium, Denmark, the Federal Republic of Germany, Finland, France, Iceland, Italy, Japan, Luxembourg, Norway, Pakistan, Spain and Sweden – provided your visit does not exceed three months and you do not take up employment.
* The Philippines and Thailand, if you hold diplomatic, official, special or service passports.

Holders of United Nations laissez-passer documents, and their wives and dependent children whose names are including in the document, can also visit Singapore visa-free provided they carry a certificate issued by the UN or the organization for which they work, stating that they are on official business.

If you are a national of an ASEAN country (Association of Southeast Asian Nations) traveling as a member of a charter group or package tour numbering not less than five persons and not more than 20, you may enter Singapore on a collective passport or travel document issued by your government. This is good only for the duration of the tour.

Nationals of all other countries (except below) can stay in Singapore for 14 days without a visa as long as they have valid passports, evidence of ample funds and firm onward passage bookings. They must leave the country within two weeks of their arrival.

Citizens of the following countries must obtain visas before arriving in Singapore: South Africa, Taiwan, Albania, Bulgaria, the People's Republic of China, Cuba, Czechoslovakia, Democratic Kampuchea, East Germany, Hungary, Laos, North Korea, Poland, Rumania, the Socialist Republic of Vietnam, the Union of Soviet Socialist Republics, and Yugoslavia. Eastern Europeans, Soviets and North Koreans with valid passports, onward bookings and entry facilities to their destination can stay for 24 hours without a visa but must leave Singapore within 24 hours of arrival.

Holders of Certificates of Identity or Affidavits and stateless persons are required to obtain visas from Singapore embassies and high commissions abroad. The visas are valid for two weeks. Where there are no Singapore missions, visa applications may be given to the office of the foreign government representative performing consular functions on behalf of the Singapore Government.

Customs regulations: Unless you are entering Singapore from Malaysia or you are under 18 years of age, you are allowed to bring in duty-free: one bottle (equivalent to one litre) either of spirits, wine, beer, stout, ale or port; and 200 cigarettes or 50 cigars or 250 gms (8 oz) of tobacco, personal effects in reasonable quantities for your regular and personal use, chocolates, cakes, biscuits not exceeding S$30 in value. Liquor and tobacco specially marked for export with the words "Singapore Duty Not Paid" and cigarettes with the prefix "E" are forbidden to be brought in.

Import authorizations are required to bring in arms and ammunitions, explosives, weapons (such as swords and krises), animals and birds (live or stuffed), meat and meat products (cooked or raw), live plants and seeds, poisons, vaccines, sera and controlled drugs, scramblers, speech inventors' online cypher equipment, walkie-talkies, transmitters, receivers, wireless microphones, radio alarms and radar equipment, books, publications, recordings and cinematographic films. If you are bringing in trade goods and items which are reasonable personal effects, you have to declare them on arrival and fill in an Onward Declaration if the value of the goods exceeds S$300.

Obtain export permits for arms, ammunition, explosives, animals, platinum, precious stones and jewelry (except those which are considered to be reasonable personal effects), poisons and drugs brought out of the country; but you don't have to pay any export duty.

You are also required to declare any dangerous weapons you are bringing in as souvenirs and hand them over to the customs. You can collect them again when you leave Singapore. A permit can be obtained for a fee from the Commissioner of Police, Arms & Explosives Branch, Blk J Kinloss House, 3 Ladyhill Road, Singapore 1025, tel: 7331000.

To import an animal or bird, apply for a permit from the Director of Primary Production (c/o City Veterinary Centre, 40 Kampong Java Road, Singapore 0922) at least two weeks before your date of arrival. Cats and dogs arriving directly from the United Kingdom, Eire, Australia and New Zealand are not subject to quarantine provided certain requirements are complied with. Cats and dogs arriving from other countries need to be vaccinated against rabies on arrival and kept in quarantine for at least 30 days at the owner's expense.

Currency: You can bring in or take out any amount of currency, banknotes, travelers cheques, stocks and bonds and other instruments of payment, but gold in any form requires an Import and Export Declaration from the Department of Trade.

When leaving the country by air, you pay an airport tax of S$12; S$5 if you are flying to Malaysia.

Health Regulations: A vaccination against yellow fever is required if you have passed through an area where yellow fever was endemic within six days of your arrival in Singapore. The vaccination requirement covers all travelers over the age of one.

Changi Airport

Changi Airport is the visitor's first contact with Singapore – if he is arriving by air – and the impression is one of modern comfort combined with the refreshing look of massed greenery and blooms (both inside and outside the terminal building) enhanced by miniature waterfalls and fountains indoors. If the arriving aircraft is parked at one of the finger piers, the passenger proceeds to the terminal building through aerobridges and horizontal travelators, then down escalators to the

The modern passenger terminal building, Changi Airport.

immigration and customs control area. If it is parked away from the terminal, a bus will take arriving passengers by bus to the Arrival Bus Station where they can proceed directly to health and immigration control. Before claiming their baggage, visitors can take advantage of the duty-free emporium at the Arrival Hall.

Other facilities include banks and money changers, post offices, telegram office, restaurants and coffee shop, car rental service and tour agencies, information and convention bureau counters, a hotel booking counter (open between 7 am and 11 pm). Left Luggage counters are located at the Arrival Hall (these are open from 10 am to 10 pm), Departure Hall (open 24 hrs a day), and the day rooms of the transit area. Charges are S$2 per bag per day; S$1.50 for each additional day. The day rooms charge S$1 per piece for a maximum of 24 hours. Be ready to open bags for security checks.

There are ramps, elevators, specially designed toilets and telephones for disabled passengers. Any passenger needing special assistance is advised to inform the airline in advance.

The Departure Hall provides day nurseries and day rooms with shower facilities for transit passengers and travelers who would like to rest or nap between flights. Enquire about rates from the desk. Singapore Airlines' smart Silver Kris Lounge for its VIPs and CIPs (Commercially Important Passengers) is equipped with shower rooms where travel-weary passengers can have a hot or cold shower, and slumberettes for a

Food stalls at Clifford Pier.

snooze or rest. There are two hospitality suites with self-service bars where passengers can help themselves to drinks, coffee, tea and snacks.

Transport to Town

If you are taking the airport bus or a taxi to town, proceed to the Arrival Crescent at the **Arrival Hall**. If you are taking a private car, go down the inclined travelators in the Arrival Hall and walk through a short tunnel to the kerbside for private cars. This is known as the **Passenger Crescent**.

Public buses run by the Singapore Bus Service Ltd (SBS) also operate regularly between Changi and bus interchanges. Information about these buses may be obtained at the passenger terminal basement.

Taxis have a flagfall of S$1.60 for the first 1.5 km (1 mile), with 10 cents for every subsequent 300 m (984 ft) and 10 cents for 45 seconds waiting time. There is an additional charge of S$3 for boarding the taxi at the airport.

Designed to meet air traffic needs into the 1990s, the construction of Changi Airport was a massive undertaking. More than 500 buildings were demolished, 4096 graves exhumed, nearly 200 hectares (494 acres) of swampland cleared, nearby hills torn down and ground leveled, low-lying areas filled up and more than 44.8 million cubic meters (58.55 million cubic yards) of sand scooped from the sea to prepare the site. It took six years of almost day and night work before phase 1 became

operational in 1981. Dominating the landscaped grounds of the airport is
a 78-m (256-ft) tall control tower.

Money

The unit of currency is the Singapore dollar, issued by the Board of
Commissioners of Currency in Singapore. Banknotes come in
denominations of $1, 5, $10, $50, $100, $500, $1000 and 10,000. Coins are
1 cent, 10, 20 and 50 cents and $1.

The approximate rates of exchange for one Singapore dollar are:

Australian dollar	0.67	Korean won	369.70
Canadian dollar	0.61	Malaysian ringgit	1.27
Deutschemark	0.84	Netherlands guilder	0.94
Irish pound	0.30	New Zealand dollar	0.75
French franc	2.85	Philippine peso	10.45
Hong Kong dollar	3.88	Sterling pound	0.26
Italian lira	624.37	Swiss franc	0.69
Japanese yen	62.68	US dollar	0.49

Banking hours are from 10 am to 3 pm Mondays to Fridays, and
9.30 am to 11.30 am on Saturdays. However, the Orchard, Katong and
Toa Payoh branches of the Development Bank of Singapore remain open
until 3 pm. Be advised that some banks do not have foreign exchange
dealings on Saturdays, or if they do, will cash only a small amount of
travelers cheques based on the previous day's rate of exchange.

Bring your passport with you when cashing travelers cheques. Bank
counters at the airport's arrival and departure halls, check-in and transit
areas stay open around the clock. Two full-service commercial banks
and a Post Office Savings Bank also operate outside the Arrival Hall.

Money changers at the airport, hotels and big shopping centers also
deal with foreign currency. Make sure they display the sign "Licensed
Money Changer".

Tipping: The practice is discouraged at the airport and in hotels and
restaurants where a service charge is already imposed. However, most
individuals like to tip if they find the service good.

Accommodation

Singapore offers the visitor a range of accommodation, from luxury
and first-class hotels run by international hotel chains to independently
operated small hotels with ambience, service hotels or apartels, and
modest, no-frills guesthouses.

At the time of writing, Singapore has 63 hotels offering more than
20,000 rooms but with the construction of new hotels and the expansion
of existing facilities, the room capacity will increase in a few year's time.
The luxury and first-class hotels offer good, personalized service

comparable to, if not better than, hotels for the same standard in Europe and North America. These have high tariffs ranging from S$175 to S$280 for singles and from S$180 to S$310 for doubles.

All the high-tariff hotels offer fully carpeted and air-conditioned guest rooms with private bath, telephone, radio, color television, and mini-refrigerator; laundry and room service; dining and entertainment facilities, swimming pool and health center (some even have a golf course, tennis and squash courts), tour and car hire desk, beauty salon, shopping arcade. Hotels add a 10% service charge and 3% to the bill.

Check-out time is 12 noon and reservations are normally held up to 6 pm, sometimes until 8 pm. There is usually no charge for children who stay with their parents in the same room, but no extra bed is provided for them. Individual hotels specify the age limit of children so accommodated. Extra beds are provided for an additional charge. The majority of the hotels are located about 15 to 20 minutes from the city center and 30 minutes from the airport.

Small and family-style hotels charging lower tariffs are also available. Some of these do not impose any service charge or government tax. They generally have a coffee shop, a restaurant and a bar but no swimming pool. There are also guesthouses, mostly on Bencoolen Street, which offers rooms without bath or air-conditioning. Some may permit the use of a communal kitchen or dining room. These may charge as little as S$25 for a single and S$30 for double.

Long-staying visitors, some of the business travelers, may prefer to stay in service flats, or apartels, which charge a monthly rate of between S$3000 and S$4,000. (For more information about hotels, turn to p.132.)

Communications

Singapore is linked to the rest of the world by satellite, 24-hour telegraph, telephone and telex facilities.

Postal services: Aerogrammes and light air letters sent anywhere in the world outside Malaysia cost 35 cents. Postcards send by air to India, Pakistan, Sri Lanka, Hong Kong and Southeast Asia cost 20 cents; to Australia, New Zealand, the Pacific Islands, Korea and Japan, 25 cents; Africa, Europe and the Middle East, 40 cents, and the Americas (including Hawaii) and the West Indies, 55 cents. For more information on letters, parcels and registered post, call the General Post Office (94531) during office hours or the Mails and Parcels Centre (2212235) after office hours. Some post offices stay open later than others.

Telephone: Local calls are free, except when made from public phone booths when each 3-minute call is charged 10 cents. International Direct Dialing (IDD) calls are charged in blocks of 6 seconds. The service operates to more than 70 destinations. Overseas calls placed through the international telephone exchange are charged for the first three minutes and subsequently for every additional minute. Dial 162 for more information.

SINGAPORE RECREATION MAP
MALAYSIA
SINGAPORE
CAUSEWAY
ADMIRALTY RD. W.
ADMIRALTY RD.
WOODLANDS RD.
MANDAI RD.
LIM CHU KANG
UPPER BUKIT TIMAH RD.
LIM CHU KANG RD.
CHOA CHU KANG RD.
CHOA CHU KANG
BUKIT PANJA
BUK PANJA
G
PAN-ISLA
JALAN BAHAR
JURONG RD.
PAN-ISLAND EXPRESSWAY
BUKIT TIMAH
Chinese Garden
Japanese Garden
JURONG
DUNEARN RD.
BUKIT TIMAH RD.
JALAN BOONLAY
UPPER AYER RAJAH RD.
G
HOLLAND RD.
UPPER JURONG RD.
J. AHMAD IBRAHIM
Jurong Bird Park
J. BUROH
CLEMENTI NEW TOWN
WEST COAST RD.
PASIR PANJANG RD.
CLEMENTI RD.
G
QUEENSWAY
FARRER
NAPIE
QUEE
G
PASIR PANJANG
AYER RAJAH RD.
ALEX AN
TK. BLANGA NEW TOWN
TELOK BLANGAH RD.
G
N
Main Road
Railway
International Boundary
Ferry
Hiking Trail
Public Beach
Park/Nature Reserve
Golf Course   G
Yacht/Sailing Club
Windsurfing
yiu

SEMBAWANG RD.
G RD.
NEE SOON
MALAYSIA
SINGAPORE
JALAN KAYU
G
PONGGOL RD.
PUNGGOL
P. UBIN
YIO CHU KANG RD.
UPPER THOMSON RD.
SERANGOON
PASIR RIS
CHANGI
LOYANG AVE.
UPPER CHANGI RD.
UPPER SERANGOON RD.
TAMPINES RD.
TAMPINES RD.
TAMPINES
Paya Lebar Airport
Changi Airport
PAYA LEBAR
BRADDELL RD.
NIE RD.
PAYA
AIRPORT RD.
TOA PAYOH
PAN- ISLAND EXPRESS WAY
CHANGI RD.
MACPHERSON RD.
PAYA LEBAR RD.
JALAN TOA PAYOH
SS WAY
BALESTIER RD.
SERANGOON RD.
PAYA LEBAR WAY
BEDOK NEW TOWN
EAST COAST PARKWAY
SCOTTS RD.
HILL ST. VICTORIA ST.
KALLANG RD.
GEYLAND RD.
KATONG
UPPER E. COAST RD.
ORCHARD RD.
GEYLANG
E. COAST RD.
MOUNT BATTEN RD.
Big Splash
CITY
NEW BRIDGE RD.
S. BRIDGE RD.
N. BRIDGE RD.
NICOLL HIGHWAY
SHENTON WAY
G RU
G
MALAYSIA
SINGAPORE
P. TEKONG

Visa and Mastercard credit cards may be used to pay for international telephone calls, telegrams and telex services at the airport service counters of the Telecommunication Authority of Singapore.

Telex: Singapore is linked by telex to more than 190 destinations. **Telegrams** can be sent to any destination, including ships at sea and in port. Outgoing international telex messages are accepted at any of the public telex booths in Telecoms Service Centres. Incoming international telex calls are accepted in telecommunications counters only in reply to an outgoing call from Singapore, and the sender must be present at the counter to collect the message. **Cables** can be sent through the hotel, the general or sub post office or any telecommunications counter.

Medical Facilities

Qualified doctors and dentists, many of them trained abroad, provide services for those who need medical attention. Most major hotels have resident doctors who are on call 24 hours a day. Just ring the Front Desk. Or look up "Medical Practitioners" and "Dental Surgeons" in the Yellow Pages of the Singapore Telephone Directory. To call an ambulance, dial 328111. The following government-run general hospitals also provide fine medical facilities:

Alexandra Hospital
Alexandra Road, tel: 635222

Singapore General Hospital
Outram Road, tel: 2223322

Toa Payoh Hospital
Toa Payoh Rise, tel: 2560411

Tan Tock Seng Hospital
Moulmein Road, tel: 2566011

Kandang Kerbau Hospital (for maternity cases)
Hampshire Road, tel: 2934044

Media

Newspapers: Singapore's daily newspapers are the English-language *Straits Times*, a morning daily founded in 1845, and *Business Times*, as well as Chinese, Malay and Tamil newspapers. Also available are international editions of foreign newspapers.

Radio: Broadcasts are conducted in the four official languages transmitted on medium wave, short-wave and FM. The English and Chinese programs commence at 6 am and end at midnight; the Malay broadcasts start at 4.45 am though midnight, and the Tamil from 6 am to 9 pm after which programs continue in the Amoy, Cantonese, Foochow,

Hakka, Hainanese and Teochew dialects until midnight. FM stereo is from 6 am to midnight.

    Television: There are two channels featuring daily programs, all of them in color. Channel 5 operates from 3 pm to midnight and Channel 8 from 6 pm to 11 pm. Programs from Malaysia can also be received on Channels 3 and 10.

Shopping

    For centuries ships laden with treasures have been calling in at Singapore which lies at the crossroads of East and West bringing in spices and silks, precious stones and prayer rugs, carpets, porcelain, lacquerware and teak. Being a free port, Singapore attracts a large variety of merchandise.

    The main tourist shopping areas are along Orchard Road, Tanglin, Scotts and Grange Roads. Orchard Road is lined with shops and department stores from end to end, displaying a wide range of merchandise. Shopping complexes include the Plaza Singapura, Specialists' Centre and Lucky Plaza; Singapore Handicraft Centre on Tanglin Road; People's Park on New Bridge Road; Chinese emporiums, stalls and stores on Arab Street, Serangoon Road and Chinatown. Some of the more posh shops and boutiques are located in hotel arcades.

    Among the better-known department stores are Tang's, housed in a Chinese-style building on Orchard Road, Robinson's at Specialists' Centre, John Little (at Specialists' Centre, Robina House on Shenton Way and Plaza Singapura), Shui Hing on Orchard Road, Isetan (on Havelock Road next to the Apollo Hotel, Liat Towers on Orchard Road, and at Changi Airport), and Yaohan at the basement of Plaza Singapura and at Thomson Plaza. The former has a supermarket selling Japanese food items and a delicatessen. Then there is the Chinese Emporium at International Building., Klasse Yu Yi on the corner of Orchard and Grange roads, Klasse Department Store, and Metro stores (on Lucky Plaza, Scotts Road, Beach Road, Penang Road and Metro Marine Parade).

What to Shop for

    Antiques: Chinese blue and white ceramics, celadon ware and glazed pottery; bronze and jade incense burners, temple wood carvings, scrolls and paintings, snuff bottles. Thai ceramics, celadon and bronzes; Indian brassware; Indonesian wooden dance masks, puppets, garuda carvings, Balinese shrine carvings; silver ornaments, brass gamelan gongs and drum sets.

    Orchard Road, Tanglin Road, Singapore Handicraft Centre and hotel shopping arcades are good places to look.

    Batiks: These come from Singapore, Indonesia and Malaysia in a selection of traditional and contemporary designs. Available as dresses,

Shopping in a hotel arcade.

skirt and blouse ensembles, men's shirts, beachwear, fashion accessories and table linens. One can also buy batik paintings.

Look for these in department stores, boutiques, Arab Street, Singapore Handicraft Centre, and, for the batik paintings, at art galleries too.

Carpets: Singapore is Southeast Asia's carpet center and is second only to London as a carpet exchange. Persian, Bokhara, Afghan, Pakistani, Indian, Turkish and Chinese rugs and carpets are found here. Visit carpet dealers and browse along Orchard Road and at the Singapore Handicraft Centre.

Fabrics: Chinese silk, Kelantan silk from northeast Malaysia (popular among the Malays for *kain songket*), Indian silks and saree materials and Thai silk are available in textile shops. The best place to look for Chinese silks are at the Chinese emporiums and Tanglin Shopping Centre and for most of the other silks in the Singapore Handicraft Centre. Philippine *jusi* and *pina* (from abaca and pineapple fibers) are sold in Filipino handicraft shops, while Indian fabrics are plentiful along Serangoon Road. Look around the People's Park complex on New Bridge Road for other fabrics.

There are several dressmakers and tailors who can turn out a Western outfit or a national costume.

Jewelry: You have a choice of unset stones – rubies and jade from Burma, smoky topaz from India, diamonds from Africa, sapphires from the Middle East, zircons from Thailand – or ready-made jewelry. For

Asian arts and crafts, Singapore Handicraft Centre.

Malay jewelry with distinctive filigree work, look at the shops along Arab Street; for Indian jewelry, go to Serangoon Road; for Chinese jewelry, the Chinese emporiums. Visit antique shops and jewelers on South Bridge Road or look at jewelers' shops in hotel shopping arcades and Singapore Handicraft Centre. Buy jewelry only from reputable shops.

Pewter: Made in Singapore pewterware comes in a range of items, both decorative and useful. You'll find it in most shopping complexes.

Reptile Skin Goods: Shoes, bags, belts, wallets, cigarette cases, briefcases made of alligator skin, crocodile, lizard or snake are sold in various locations. When in doubt, go to the Singapore Handicraft Centre.

At department stores with fixed prices, bargaining is not the done thing; but in places like Arab Street, Serangoon Road, or other bazaars, bargaining is accepted practice. This must be conducted in the most polite way, suggesting to the shopkeeper that his price might be too high and asking him to reduce a little bit. You may or may not get what you bargained for. But you may get some concession.

Singapore Handicraft Centre

If you enjoy watching artisans at work – weaving, carving, painting, batik printing, embroidering – then the place to go is the Singapore Handicraft Centre on Tanglin Road. Open from 10 am to 8 pm daily, the demonstrations take place between 11 am and 1 pm and 3 pm and 5 pm

You could chance upon craftsmen polishing gems or lacquer ornaments; making papier-mâché products; carving jade or rosewood furniture, painting a ceremonial mask, engraving pewter, or making fashion accessories from reptile skin.

The arts and crafts of Afghanistan, Australia, China, Hong Kong, India, Indonesia, Iran, Japan, Malaysia, Pakistan, the Philippines, Singapore, Sri Lanka, Taiwan, Thailand, and Vietnam are represented here. Singapore, indeed, lives up to its name of Instant Asia under this roof. For those who are not visiting other Asian countries, this is a good browsing place to pick up a souvenir or two. They are not only decorative, some are also useful and make unusual gift items as well.

You don't have to travel all the way to Sri Lanka to buy the devil masks which Ambalangoda is famous for. Nor do you have to go to Bali for *garuda* and *barong* carvings; to West Java for *wayang kulit* and *wayang golek* puppets; to Kelantan for kites; to Kashmir for jewelry boxes made of papier mâché and mirror-work embroidery; to the Philippines for lovely mother-of-pearl plates and shell jewelry; to Sabah for their indigenous crafts. You can find them all at the Singapore Handicraft Centre, along with Afghan and Persian prayer rugs, Kadazan dolls and jewelry, Sarawak pottery, Thai bronze and brass tableware, Nonya embroidery, Bangladeshi and Pakistani embroidered textiles.

Advice to shoppers: Don't listen to touts. When buying expensive items, look around first and compare prices and brands. Examine the goods carefully before buying. Once purchased, items are not returnable or exchangeable. Insist on a receipt which accurately describes what you have bought, stating serial number, brand name, price in Singapore dollars, date purchased. Receipts for jewelry should state the carat and percentage of precious metal, and for antiques one should have in addition a certificate stating its age. Complaints should be sent in writing to Singapore Tourist Promotion Board, Raffles City Tower, 250 North Bridge Road #36-04 Singapore 0617.

Transport

Moving about in Singapore is easy and convenient as the island is linked by an excellent network of roads, motorways, and flyovers. Traffic moves on the left.

Bus: The cheapest way to move about is by bus, which reaches even the remotest parts of the island. Buses normally run from 6 am to 11.30 pm. Fares range from 40 to 80 cents. Buses do not automatically pick up passengers at every stop, so hail your bus from the bus stop if you want to get aboard. Have ready plenty of loose change or the exact fare, if possible. This is especially useful when traveling during peak hours as conductors don't have time to change big notes.

Some buses are one-man operated; these display the sign "OMO". Have exact fare ready as they charge either a flat rate of 80 cents or a fare of 40, 60, or 80 cents depending upon where you board the bus. The fare is usually posted on the signboard in front of the bus.

Some bus stops have a board indicating the destination and the bus number serving that route. You may also buy a bus guide from a bookshop or a newsstand. If in doubt, call the Public Relations Office of the Singapore Bus Service (Tel: 2872727) during office hours (8 am to 4.30 pm weekdays, and up to 12.30 pm Saturdays).

Hire Car: There are a number of hire-car companies. For a listing, look in the Yellow pages of the telephone directory. Mileage charges work out at around 15 to 95 cent per kilometer (0.62 mile). Air-conditioned chauffeur-driven cars rent from S$20 to 40 per hour. The daily rate is S$160-320, as against the daily rate of S$42-195 for the self-drive car. Weekly rates range from S$1120 to S$2240 for chauffeur-driven cars, compared with the weekly S$252-1080 for self-driven cars.

The Central Business District (CBD) of Singapore is a restricted zone during the morning peak hours of 7.30 am to 10.15 am. Mondays to Saturdays except public holidays. Cars or taxis entering this traffic-controlled zone must purchase and display area licences. The cost of a daily area licence is S$5.

If you park in a car park managed by the Urban Redevelopment Authority (URA) or the Housing Development Board (HDB), you must display a parking coupon indicating the date and parking time on the window or windscreen of your car. Parking coupons, sold in booklets with different denominations (40 cents, 80 cents and S$1.60), can be bought in advance from HDB area offices. URA parking kiosks, post offices, and some petrol stations. The coupons can be used interchangeably in URS or DB parking areas. For rules and regulations on driving in Singapore, contact the nearest police station or the Automobile Station of Singapore, tel: 7372444, open from 9 am to 5 pm on weekdays and until 1 pm on Saturdays.

Taxis: There are more than 9,000 licensed taxis in Singapore, all equipped with meters. Extra charges are levied for each passenger exceeding two (babies not counted), and 10 cents for every piece of luggage other than hand luggage. There's also a surcharge of 50% of the metered fare from 1 am to 6 am.

Make sure your taxi displays an area licence if you have to go to the Central Business District during the restricted hours. If the taxi has no area licence, you or the driver can either pay for it (S$2), or alternatively, agree to share the taxi with two other passengers. Do not hail a taxi along double yellow lines or other than at a taxi stand in the Central Business District. Most shopping centers have taxi ranks clearly indicated outside their main entrances. Dial-a-taxi service is available by telephoning 4525555, 2933111, or 2500700. You pay an additional 40 cents if you engage a taxi by phone.

Indicate your destination when you board the taxi and make sure the meter is down. Beware of drivers who promise to take you to reliable stores and then overcharge you by taking the long route. If you have any complaints (or commendations), note the taxi registration number, the time and place of boarding, and report it to the Registry of Vehicles, Sin Ming Drive, 2057, tel: 4594222 or the Singapore Tourist Promotion Board, Raffles City Tower, 250 North Bridge Road #36-04 Singapore 0617.

Trishaws: These are nothing but bicycles equipped with side cars, and operated solely by leg power. Trishaws are popular in some Oriental cities but as a mode of transport in a city dominated by motor vehicles, they can be daunting for the faint of heart.

Establish the price before you board the trishaw. The going rate is around S$30 for two hours but you can haggle them down to S$20 if you are good at bargaining.

Cable cars: A cable car system connects the main island of Singapore with the small resort island of Sentosa, carrying a maximum of 700 passengers an hour in any one direction. Each cabin comfortably seats six adults. The crossing takes 13 minutes from Mount Faber station, affording panoramic views. Hours of operation are from 10 am to 7 pm Mondays to Saturdays, and 9am to 7pm on Sundays and public holidays. Round-trip fare for an adult is S$7 and a child S$3.50. The last car leaves Sentosa at 7pm.

Ferries: Regular ferry services operate between the mainland and the offshore islands such as Sentosa, Kusu and St. John's. The ferry terminal is located at the World Trade Centre.

Tourist Guides

If you are on a privately arranged tour, use only the services of tourist guides licensed by the Singapore Tourist Promotion Board. These guides wear special badges and must be able to produce their licences when requested. Guides who conduct tours in English, Mandarin, Malay and Tamil are paid S$8.50 an hour while guides who conduct tours in other foreign languages charge S$17 an hour. Prices change, however, so check first with the STPB.

Other Services

There are many barbershops and beauty salons providing a full range of beauty services and treatments, from a simple shampoo and blow-dry to haircuts, perming, tinting, and facials. Unless you know of a particular hairdresser, your best chance is to go to the hotel barbershop or salon. Most first-class hotels will lend hair dryers to guests. Just dial Housekeeping and ask to borrow one. This saves you the trouble of lugging around your own hair dryer and adapters.

Contrast between old and new.

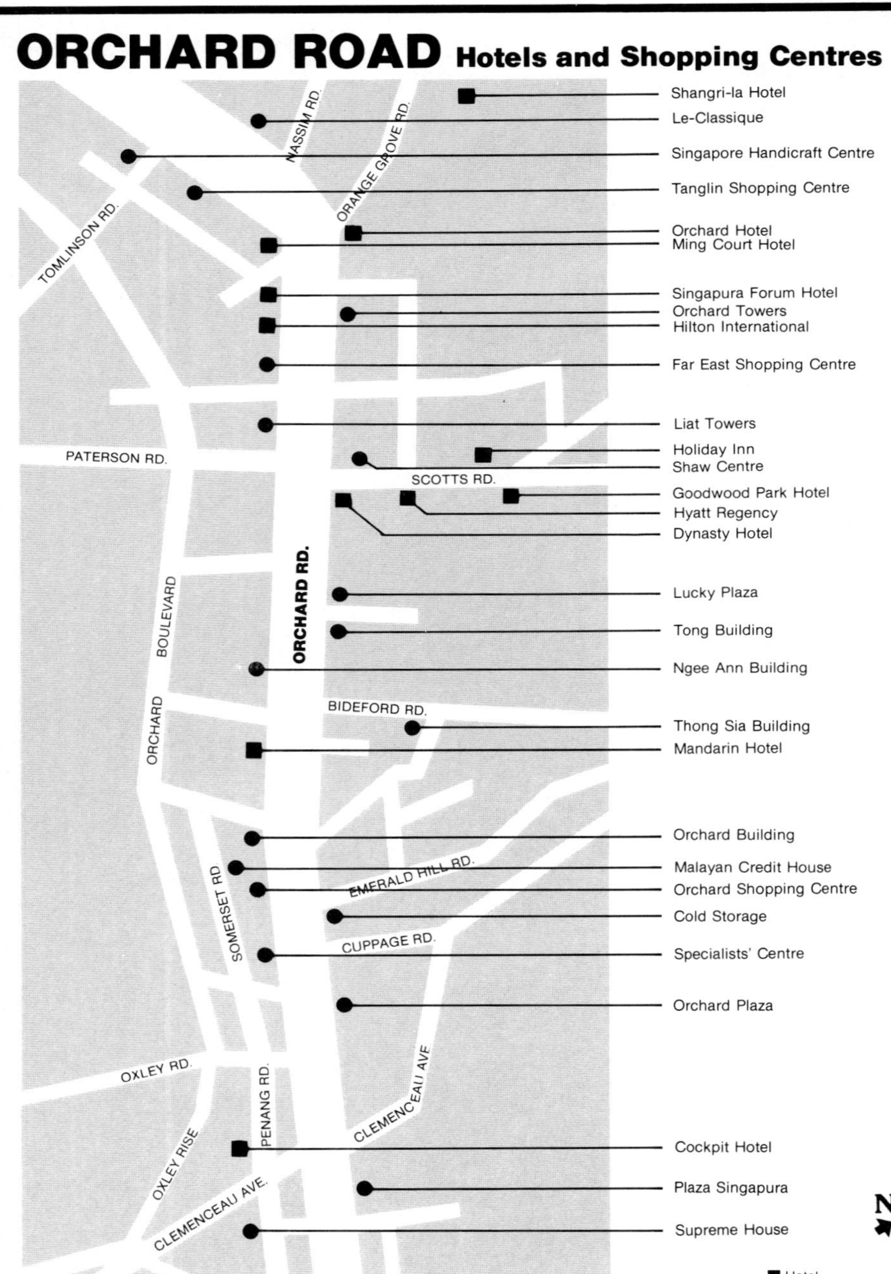

ORCHARD ROAD Hotels and Shopping Centres
NASSIM RD.
ORANGE GROVE RD.
TOMLINSON RD.
PATERSON RD.
SCOTTS RD.
BOULEVARD
ORCHARD RD.
ORCHARD
BIDEFORD RD.
SOMERSET RD
EMERALD HILL RD.
CUPPAGE RD.
OXLEY RD.
PENANG RD.
CLEMENCEAU AVE.
OXLEY RISE
CLEMENCEAU AVE.
Shangri-la Hotel
Le-Classique
Singapore Handicraft Centre
Tanglin Shopping Centre
Orchard Hotel
Ming Court Hotel
Singapura Forum Hotel
Orchard Towers
Hilton International
Far East Shopping Centre
Liat Towers
Holiday Inn
Shaw Centre
Goodwood Park Hotel
Hyatt Regency
Dynasty Hotel
Lucky Plaza
Tong Building
Ngee Ann Building
Thong Sia Building
Mandarin Hotel
Orchard Building
Malayan Credit House
Orchard Shopping Centre
Cold Storage
Specialists' Centre
Orchard Plaza
Cockpit Hotel
Plaza Singapura
Supreme House
N
Hotel
Shopping Centre
yiu

Electricity. Power is delivered in 220-240 volts at 50 cycles, but most hotels are equipped with step-down transformers.

Photography. Film is readily available and relatively inexpensive. Color film can be processed in 24 hours; black and white in eight. As a matter of courtesy, ask permission before taking photos of people and places of worship.

Lost and Found

If your luggage is missing or you have lost something on the aircraft, get in touch with your airline or the ground handling companies. Or call Singapore Airport Terminal Services (SATS), tel: 5418888 or Changi International Airport Services (CIAS), tel: 5421234.

The Airport Management division of the Department of Civil Aviation has a Lost and Found office on the third floor of the passenger terminal building. Enquire from them if you have lost anything within the airport.

If you have left something behind in a taxi or bus, write to the Lost and Found Section, Registry of Vehicles, Sin Ming Drive, 2057, tel: 4594222.

Complaints

Address any complaint – be it against a taxi driver or a shopkeeper – to the Singapore Tourist Promotion Board, Raffles City Tower, 250 North Bridge Road #36-04 Singapore 0617.

Sport and Recreation

There is a wide range of sporting activities and facilities maintained by private clubs and by the Singapore Sports Council (SSC) which a visitor or a resident can take advantage of. Singaporeans are particularly fond of jogging, swimming and playing football; popular times for these sports are the early mornings and late afternoons.

The Singapore Sports Council manages and maintains the National Stadium complex, athletic centers, multipurpose playing fields and pitches, a mini golf-course, indoor stadia, swimming complexes, netball courts, squash and tennis courts, a swimming lagoon, and fitness corners and parks.

East Coast Park

One of the most popular recreation areas in Singapore – patronized by residents and tourists alike – is East Coast Park. This huge complex is built on reclaimed land alongside the expressway that connects Changi Airport with the business district. Various sports activities are offered here: swimming, windsurfing, tennis, squash, biking, and the

ever-popular kite-flying. Kite-flying festivals are regularly held, and
Singapore recently hosted an international kite-flying contest which
feature the biggest and most unusual kites in the world.

Undoubtedly one of the biggest attractions in the park, particularly
for families, is the **Big Splash**, a 50 m (164 ft) water slide at the edge of
the pool. Be careful, though. Women with itsy-bitsy bikinis have been
known to be embarrassed when sliding down this ramp. Tickets are S$3
for adults; S$2 for children. The Big Splash is open from 10 am to 9 pm
daily except Mondays.

There is also a man-made lagoon, built at a cost of S$4 million and
said to be equivalent in size to 40 Olympic-sized swimming pools. Six
thousand bathers can splash to their heart's content without making the
place too crowded.

Courses in **windsurfing** are conducted at the East Coast Sailing
Centre. The basic course consists of two three-hour sessions at S$75 per
course. The hours of instruction are from 10 am to 1 pm and from 2 pm to
5 pm. Surfboards can be rented by non-members between 9 am and
6.30 pm for S$10 an hour; S$35 for four hours, and S$60 for eight hours.

At the **Singapore Tennis Centre**, non-members may play at S$6 per
hour between 7 am and 6 pm; S$8 per hour from 6 pm to 11 pm and on
Sundays and public holidays. To obtain a court during weekends, it is
necessary to book a week ahead.

Golfers can practise their swing at the **Parkland Golf Driving
Range**, open to the public from 7.30 am to 10 pm daily. The 200-m
(656-ft) long range has 60 bays, and you can hire clubs for S$2.50 each.
The fee is S$4 for 100 balls on weekdays between 7.30 am and 3.30 pm
and S$5 between 3.30 pm and 10 pm and on Sundays and public
holidays. By arrangement with the club, aspiring golfers can receive
instruction at S$12 for 30 minutes. All prices are likely to be revised, so
check first.

The park has a **Crocodilarium** which breeds crocodiles for their
hide. Open daily from 9 am to 5.10 pm.

The park also has a coffee shop and a hawker center with about 60
stalls offering a variety of drinks and food such as duck rice, *laksa, satay,
beehoon,* and egg curry puff.

Golf

Singapore is a part of the Far East Professional Circuit which
includes Malaysia, Hong Kong and the Philippines, and has some fine
golf courses. The resort island of **Sentosa** has an 18-hole, par 71
championship course. The 165-m (541-ft) par-three second hole is on
a tiny offshore reef which you can reach only by a bridge. If your
drive is poor, you will see your ball heading straight for the sea.
There is another golf course, par 72, on the island. Non-members

Cricket at the Padang: continuing an old British tradition.

are welcome to play there (Tel: 4722722) at S$50 on weekdays, more on weekends and public holidays. The **Jurong Country Club** (Jurong Town Hall Road, tel 5605655), **Sembawang Country Club** (Sembawang Road, tel: 2574714) and **Tanglin Golf Course** (Minden Road, tel: 637236) also accept non-members. Advance booking is required at the Sembawang Country Club. At **Changi Golf Club** (Netheravon Road, tel: 5451298) and **Singapore Island Country Club** (Upper Thomson road, tel: 4592222) non-members may play only on weekdays. Green fees range from S$5 per game (Tanglin) to S$70 (Island Club) while caddy fees are from S$4 (Changi) to S$10 (Island).

Bowling

There are several bowling alleys most of which have the latest equipment. These include: **Jackie's Bowl** (located at Katong, tel: 416519 and Orchard, tel: 7374744), **Kalang Bowl** (Tel: 4460545), **Pasir Panjang Bowl** (Tel: 7755555), **Plaza Bowl** (Tel: 2824821), and **Starbowl** (Tel: 3381421). One game before 6 pm costs about S$1.80, going up to S$2 after six and on weekends.

Squash, Tennis and Badminton

These are very popular and there are many courts where you can enjoy these sports. You can play squash and tennis at the **Alexandra Park** (Tel: 637236), **Farrer Park** (Tel: 2514166), **Changi** (Tel: 5452941), **National Stadium** in Kallang (Tel: 4408622), and **Seletar** on The Oval (Tel: 4814745). In addition, squash enthusiasts can also play at the **Singapore Squash Centre** in Central Park (Tel: 3360155). A half-hour session in a non air-conditioned squash court costs about S$1.50 while a 30-minute session in an air-conditioned court may cost between S$2 and S$2.50 depending on the day and time of day. Other tennis courts are located on Deptford Road (**Sembawang Tennis Courts**), Sherwood Road (**Tanglin Tennis Courts**) and East Coast Park (**Singapore Tennis Centre**). A game of tennis costs from S$2 to S$7 per hour per court, depending on the day and time of day. It is sometimes necessary to book courts in advance.

Horseback Riding, Horse Racing and Polo

The **Polo Club** on Thomson Road offers equestrians the chance to ride as well as watch polo games, while the **Singapore Turf Club** on Bukit Timah Road is the venue for horse races. Inquiries may also be made from the Turf Club regarding horseback riding with the **Saddle Club** (Tel: 662264).

Water Sports

The hot tropical climate of Singapore encourages water sports, and swimming, water-skiing and boating are very popular. Sentosa is easily one of the most popular places for various types of water sports. Its accessibility from the mainland (it only takes about 12 minutes by ferry to get there) adds to its popularity. On its southern coastline is a swimming lagoon, about 1.2 km (0.75 mile) long and 137 km (85 miles) wide. Visitors can swim or go boating. Pedal and rowboats are available for a small fee. Adjacent to the swimming lagoon is the **Canoe Centre,** another lagoon of approximately the same size, which was created for windsurfing and canoeing. You can hire fiberglas canoes which are either single-seater or double-seater. Windsurfing enthusiasts can also rent sailboards. On the island's eastern end is **Siloso Beach** which also caters for swimmers as well as those who just want to sunbathe.

While the major hotels, private clubs and swimming complexes run by the Singapore Sports Council offer swimming facilities, those in search of something more exciting can try the Big Splash at the **East Coast Park** (Tel: 2451211) or, for the less adventurous, the **Mitsukoshi Gardens** in Jurong (9 Japanese Garden Road, Jurong Water Sports Complex, tel: 2614771), open 10 am to 6 pm on weekdays and 9 am to 8 pm on weekends. Family outings are held in these parks.

Ponggol, at the northern tip of the island, with its land-locked coves and bays and glassy smooth waters also attracts boating enthusiasts. Boats and water-skis can be hired from the Ponggol Boatel (Tel: 882788). You can also engage motorized boats, called bumboats, from Clifford Pier or Jardine Steps to take you to the palm-fringed southern islands such as Kusu, Sisters, St. John's and Hantu for a day of swimming and sunbathing.

Snorkeling and scuba diving are two water sports which are attracting a growing number of adherents. Under the Singapore Underwater Federation, an affiliate of the World Underwater Federation, diving expeditions and instructions are held. There are now 17 diving clubs and assorted shops selling diving equipment or offering instructions which are members of the SUF. For those interested in scuba-diving, clubs such as the **Singapore Sub Aqua Club** (Tel: 4690944), the Metropolitan YMCA and several community centers are open to the public who want to join them.

If you are interested in sailing enquire from the **Changi Sailing Club** (Tel: 5454322) and the **Singapore Yacht Club** (Tel: 2651453).

If flying is your thing, get in touch with the **Singapore Flying Club** (Tel: 4810200/4810502). You can soar aboard a Cessna, Piper or Twin Comanche.

Offshore Islands

There are 42 offshore islands ringing Singapore. Of these, about 25 are inhabited; the rest are no more than sandbanks.

Eight of the inhabited islands are in various stages of development as holiday resorts. The foremost of these resorts is Sentosa, to the south of Singapore. But there are also others: Buran Darat, Kusu (Tortoise

The monorail at Sentosa.

Island), St. John's, Sisters, Pulau Hantu (Ghost Island) all on the south; Pulau Seleter and Teremby Retan Laut, off the northern and western costs of mainland Singapore.

Sentosa

For fun and sun, Singaporeans – and visitors – go to Sentosa, a 375-hectare (926 acres) island resort just minutes away from the mainland. There you can play golf, go swimming, canoeing, windsurfing, sunbathing, sightseeing, cycling, hiking, jogging, pony-riding or roller-skating. There is a campsite with tents for hire, barbecue pits for picnics and a 162-room hotel with conference facilities.

Before World War II the island was known as **Pulau Blakang Mati** ("the island of leaving death behind") and functioned as a fortress and a military base for the British until they withdrew their forces from Singapore in 1967. In the 1970s it was developed as a holiday resort and renamed Sentosa. In Malay this means "The Isle of Peace and Tranquillity".

To get there: a regular ferry service from the World Trade Centre gives you easy access to the island. Ferries operated by the Singapore Port Authority, leave at 15-minute intervals between 7 am and 11 pm from Mondays to Thursday. Last departure from Sentosa back to Singapore is at 10.45 pm Many tour operators offer day and evening packages tours to Sentosa. Pick up can be arranged from major hotels by local tour agents.

Cable cars ply between the mainland and Senotsa.

Once on the island, you can take advantage of the monorail service (9 am to 10 pm) to do your sightseeing. You can get off or board at any of the stops in the 6.1 km (3.8 mile) route. You can also hike, or bike. The 4.25 km (2.64 mile) **bicycle track** leads you to various attractions on the island, passing through woods and along the beach. Bicycles can be hired for a minimum of three hours at the Sentosa ferry terminal or at the swimming lagoon. The deposit is refundable. The bicycle kiosk is open from 9 am to 5 pm. There is an extra charge for overnight rental.

For those who wish to ride ponies, there are two **riding tracks**: one for beginners, another for more experienced riders. Riding lessons are also available.

There is a huge **roller-skating rink** (12,000 sq m / 14,354 sq yd, reportedly the largest of its kind in Southeast Asia) capable of accommodating 1000 skaters. Beginners can skate in the smaller section comprising 700 sq m (837 sq yd). The rink is floodlit for night skaters. A spectators' gallery seats 600. There is a small charge for renting skates and battery-operated car for children. Admission to the rink is free.

Swimmers have a choice of three places: a protected **swimming lagoon** 800 m (2,624 ft) long, and the **Siloso** and **Bukit Nanas** beaches. The swimming lagoon is divided into two: the western lagoon for swimming and boating, and the eastern lagoon for canoeing and windsurfing. Double-seater canoes and sailboards can be rented by the hour. There is a deposit which is refundable. Dinghies, deck chairs,

pedal boats, beach umbrellas and lockers can also be rented by the hour
or by the day.

Golfers can play on the 18-hole par-71 championship golf course on
the southwestern tip of the island, covering an area of 60.7 hectares
(150 acres). one of its interesting features is the second hole green which
is a reclaimed offshore reef. Concessionary rates for green fees are given
to guests of the Apollo Sentosa Hotel. Make arrangements with the golf
club (Tel: 4722722), open from 7.30 am to 5 pm Mondays to Saturdays,
and up to 8 pm on Sundays and Public Holidays. Golfers are ferried for
free from the World Trade Centre (platform 1) to Serapong Jetty on
Sentosa and a golf club bus transports them to the club. Clubs and shoes
can be hired from the club.

Other places of interest on the island are the Maritime Museum, the
Coralarium, Fort Siloso and the Wax Museum – all accessible by monorail.

The **Maritime Museum** depicts the history and development of the
Port of Singapore – one of the world's busiest – in its Port of Singapore
Gallery. The Primitive Craft Gallery shows the evolution of watercraft
and exhibits models and several full-sized primitive watercraft. The
Fisheries Gallery shows various methods of fishing and fishing devices
used in Singapore. Visitors can also watch boats being built in the Boat
Building Shed next to the Fisheries Galleries.

The **Coralarium** shows a spectacular display inside an
air-conditioned coral cave of various types of incandescent living corals
and dangerous marine invertebrates from the seas of Singapore.
Stag-horn coral, slipper coral, brain coral, honeycomb coral, are just
some of the fascinating corals to be seen. Also on view are stone fish, lion
fish, cat fish, puffer fish, sting-rays, sea snakes and sea urchins. The
World of Shells shows more than 2000 seashells, among them the rare
Glory of the Sea, the Cone of Bengal, Golden Cowrie and Rose Murex.
Dominating the 1.2 hectares (3 acres) of land on which the Coralarium
stands is an 18-m (59-ft) high coral tower.

Fort Siloso has been preserved as a historic zone on the island. Until
1967 it was used as a British garrison. Built in the 1880s to guard the
western approaches to the harbor of Singapore, it is the only one of the
four forts constructed to defend the harbor against hostile vessels which
has not been destroyed. The four-hectare (ten acres) complex that makes
up the fort consists of underground tunnels, gun emplacements,
ammunition bunkers and searchlight posts, machine-gun posts and
barracks for the soldiers. On the grounds may also be seen miniature
specimens of Malay cannons and hand weapons which include parangs,
kris, Dayak knives, blow-pipes, cross bows and watch locks.

The **Sentosa Wax Museum**, formerly called the Surrender Chamber,
contains two tableaux in wax as well as a picture gallery. The Japanese
surrender to the Allied Forces on 12 September 1945 shows 27 life-sized
figures created by Josephine Tussaud International. The surrender

document was signed by Admiral Lord Louis Mountbatten, Supreme Commander of Southeast Asia for the Allies,and General Seishiro Itagaki, Supreme Commander of the Japanese Forces in Southeast Asia, for the Japanese. The tableau was originally displayed at the City Hall where the actual surrender took place but was transferred to Sentosa in 1975.

The other wax tableau is that of the British surrendering to the Japanese on 15 February 1942 at the Ford Motors Boardroom. There are 15 life-sized wax figures created by CPA of Tokyo. General A.E. Percival, General Officer Commanding Malaya, and Lt General Tomoyoki Yamashita, Commander-in-Chief, Japanese Forces Malaya, are the leading personalities. This exhibit was opened to the public in 1981. Augmenting the tableaux are sound recordings which give a poignant touch to the scenes.

Other attractions on Sentosa are the **Sentosa Art Centre** near the Carlton Hill cable car station which displays works of art by local Singaporean artists, sculptors and calligraphers and also holds regular art demonstrations and the **musical fountain** built on the reclaimed site of Imbiah Bay. This consists of a swan-shaped pool, two terrace pools and a viewing gallery accommodating 1000 persons. The fountain shoots up to a height of 30 m (99 ft), visible from the World Trade Centre across the waters. The spectacular water display shows sixteen basic formations, enhanced by the play of lights and musical themes such as *Oklahoma, My Fair Lady, Singapura*, etc. There are three evening shows on week nights; more on weekends and public holidays.

There are food kiosks all over the island which sell packed lunches and dinners. The **Rasa Sentosa** food center, located between the ferry terminal and the musical fountain, offers open-air dining facilities. Beneath gaily colored umbrellas patrons can order seafood or regional specialities with a complement of fresh fruits and fruit juices. The hawkers were chosen by an SDC food-tasting committee so that only the best hawker food is served here.

Accommodation on the island depends on the individual's choice. There are holiday camps for those who want to rough it, a youth hostel and a hotel: Campbeds and tents can be hired. There is a deposit made upon booking that is refundable unless the booking is canceled less than seven days before the proposed date of occupancy. The **youth hostel** is fully furnished with 20 bedrooms for groups of five, ten, fifteen or twenty persons. The hostel includes a lounge, dining room, kitchen and toilet. There is a refundable deposit for booking. For enquiries call Sentosa Information Office, tel: 2707888. **The Apollo Sentosa Hotel** has 162 chalets and rooms. Facilities include swimming pools, squash and tennis courts, a restaurant serving Western and Chinese food, a 900-seat convention hall and sauna and massage. Call 4734388 for further details and reservations. To charter transport within Sentosa, contact the Sentosa Transport Office on 3397738 or 2353111.

九華塔

Kusu

Kusu, also known as **Tortoise Island** because of its turtle shape, lies six kilometers (four miles) south of Singapore. It consists of a main island connected to an islet by a short isthmus. On the main island is **a Malay shrine** or *Kramat* while on the islet is a **Chinese temple** dedicated to Tua Pek Kong, god of prosperity. Except for one month of the year, Kusu is a sleepy little island, ideal for getting away from the crowds and just relaxing on the beach or swimming. Reclamation projects have created two beaches on the northern and southern sides of the island, each enclosed by a swimming lagoon. There are picnic shades, changing rooms and a few food stalls, but bring your own picnic lunch if you decide to make a day of it.

Many legends surround this island. One legend tells of a turtle that turned itself into an island to give refuge to the passengers of a floundering ship. Another legend says a giant turtle saved shipwrecked Chinese and Malay fishermen from drowning by carrying them on its back until they reached land. In gratitude they built shrines to their deities on the island.

Pilgrims flock to Kusu during the month of September or October with yellow ribbons on their wrists to pray for prosperity, fertility and good luck. After praying, a supplicant ties a stone (symbolizing his particular wish) to a tree. If his prayer is answered, he goes back to the island on the next pilgrimage season to untie the stone.

Four ferries a day ply between the Ferry Terminal Building at the World Trade Centre to Kusu; more on weekends and public holidays.

St. John's

This is practically next door to Kusu, but is larger and more frequented by holidaymakers. There are three large swimming lagoons with clear waters bordered by rocky outcrops, and shower and changing rooms. In addition to swimming, one can also play basketball and tennis on the island. To book a tennis court and for enquiries, call **St. John's Island Camp Office**, 414115 between 9 am and 4.30 pm. There are cafeterias on the island (for provisions and enquiries, call 2569409) but it is best to bring your own food along.

Accommodation is available by hiring holiday bungalows, holiday camps or day camps. Fully-furnished and self-contained two- and three-bedroom bungalows for four to six persons have a lounge, dining room, kitchen and annex. Holiday camps provide cooking, sleeping and bathing facilities. For enquiries regarding bungalows and day camps, call Sentosa Information Office, 2707888, and for holiday camps call the People's Association, 3440873.

The Cloud-Piercing Pagoda, Chinese Garden, Jurong.

Four ferries a day make the trip to St John, stopping off at Kusu. It is possible to visit the two islands on the same ticket which costs $5 return.

Sisters

These are two uninhabited, thickly wooded islands looking very similar to each other with swimming beaches and lagoon. Each island is ringed by a coral reef, popular among divers. The facilities are rather limited: just beach shelters and changing huts. Located nine kilometers (5.6 miles) from the mainland, it takes about an hour to reach the islands by bumboat which can be arranged through the Port Authority ticket office at the World Trade Centre. A group of 10 to 12 persons can easily get a boat, but lesser numbers should join a group going to the island that day. It costs around S$100 return per boat to Sisters Islands or Pulau Hantu.

Pulau Hantu

This is actually called **Ghost Island**, located about 45 minutes' away by boat from the mainland. Swimming, fishing and scuba diving are its main attractions for weekenders and day-trippers. The island has three swimming lagoons with changing and shower facilities. Bring a picnic baskets if you intend to stay the day.

Buran Darat

Just 300 m (984 ft) east of Sentosa is Buran Darat, a flat sandbank which has been converted into a holiday resort and landscaped. It has a wide swimming lagoon and other bathing areas. Bumboats (S$60 return per boat carrying 12 passengers) can be hired from bumboat operators at Jardine Steps, three minute's walk from the World Trade Centre.

Arts and Entertainment

Cultural shows, dramatic presentations, art and literary exhibitions, films, disco-dancing, dinner-theatre, cabaret – take your pick. There's something for everyone. It may be that you are in Singapore when the city is holding its Festival of Arts, Festival of Choirs, Drama Festival, Concerts for the Young, or celebrating a special religious or ethnic festival. Get a copy of the tourist publications given free to visitors in the major hotels to see what's on, or contact the Singapore Tourist Promotion Board (STPB), tel: 3396622. If music is your cup of tea, consult the programs at the **Victoria Concert Hall**. There are regular concerts performed by the Singapore Symphony Orchestra or visiting orchestras, solo recitals by young Singaporean instrumentalists and chamber music by local and foreign ensembles. Free Sunday afternoon band concerts are also held at the Botanic Gardens from 5.30 to 6.30 pm.

Cultural Shows

Two cultural offerings especially designed to give visitors an introduction to Singapore are shown at the **Singapore Cultural Theatre** on Grange Road, close to the STPB offices on Tanglin Road.

Instant Asia is a mixture of Chinese, Indian and Malay dances and music, complete with a Lion Dance, an excerpt from a Chinese opera, an exhibition of Oriental martial arts and snake charmers coaxing snakes out of baskets. As a souvenir, you can have a photograph of yourself with a python obligingly curled round your neck. *Singapore Experience* is an audio-visual presentation of the history and people, the sounds and sights of Singapore using a quadraphonic soundtrack and commentary and 56 projectors to flash some 4,480 slides onto a wide 10-panel screen. Both last for 45 minutes. Showings of the former are held in the mornings from 9.30 am; the latter in the afternoons from midday. Admission for adults is S$5.

Chinese Opera

One of the most popular forms of entertainment is the Chinese *Wayang*, the Malay term used to apply to Chinese street opera. These productions are performed on makeshift wooden stages erected on the streets during festivals. Wooden seats are provided for the audience.

For a person who has not been brought up in the tradition of the Chinese opera, it may be difficult to understand what's going on. The music may sound strange, more like cacophony, the falsetto and high-pitched voices grating to the ear. In fact the music is highly developed and complex. Chinese string and percussion instruments, and occasionally flutes, provide not only the musical accompaniment but also the timing for every movement on stage, from walking to gesturing with hands. The music binds together the singing and acting.

There are many types of Chinese opera and the skills are passed on from generation from generation. Costumes and make-up are elaborate, often indicating the type of character portrayed. By contrast, stage settings are very simple and objects like tables and chairs, banners and scarves, etc. may be used symbolically to depict mountains, rivers and streams.

Plots are based on literary plays and love stories; or they may recreate legends and historical episodes. Of course it helps to know the storyline before seeing the opera.

Do not expect to see a full Chinese opera on street corners at any time of the year. They are staged on special occasions only, such as during festivals. Contact the Tourist Board for exact locations of opera performances during festival times.

Cinema

There are more than 75 air-conditioned cinema houses showing Western, Chinese, Malay and Tamil films. Admission prices range from

S$1.50 to S$3.50. There are five showings daily, starting at 11 am. The last show is at 9.15 pm. However, on Saturdays and the eve of public holidays, an additional show is held at midnight. Smoking is prohibited in the cinemas.

After-dark Entertainment

Gone are the transvestites who used to enliven a still dawn in Bugis Street. Like the hawkers and food vendors, this segment of humanity has been relocated. They now ply their trade in less obvious places. The fact is, Singapore authorities don't want tourists to associate nightlife with Bugis Street. After all, they believe, there are other more interesting places to go to and things to do.

Practically all the hotels have their own bars and cocktail lounges where people can go for a drink before or after dinner. Music is often provided by an instrumentalist (either a pianist, violinist or a guitarist), a vocalist or a small band. In most entertainment establishments, a 3% government tax and 10% service charge is added to your bill.

Most nightspots stay open until 1 or 2 am, later during weekends.

Discos

If disco is your thing, the hotels' nightspots are your scene. Juliana-style discos are in and the smart set dance to the music of the tops in pops and the latest in the hit parade. A few accept members only and hotel guests; others impose a cover charge for non-members. Some boast London-trained disc jockeys. Special lights, laser beams, mirrors, sound effects, chatty D.J.'s, distinctive decor are all part of the scene. Dress is casual.

Among the well-rated private clubs are the **Chinoiserie** at the Hyatt Regency, **The Club** at the Marco Polo, **El Marocco** at the Oberoi Imperial, **The Library** at the Mandarin and the **West End Club** at the Goodwood Park. You may dance, read a magazine, play backgammon or chess or just sit at the bar. A cover charge may be included in the price of the first drink.

Among the discos which are open to the public are **Xanadu** at Shangri-La, **Studio M** at Merlin Hotel and **Black Velvet Club** at the Century Park Sheraton. Music from mixers or live bands is non-stop. A cover charge may be included in the price of the first drink or imposed separately.

Dinner Shows

The city's major hotels also stage cultural shows as part of a buffet or set dinner or outdoor barbecue by the poolside, while theater-restaurants offer, along with ethnic cuisine, local floorshows and dancing. Cost of dinner and show may range from S$30 to S$40,

Chinese opera, a popular form of folk entertainment.

inclusive of tax and service charge. Prices change, however, so you may find that costs have gone up considerably. The **Raffles Hotel**, a landmark in Singapore, offers a show with Malay dances; the **Mandarin** a poolside *Asean Night* with barbecue; the **Hyatt Regency**, *Malam Singapura* with barbecue dinner poolside. Most dinners start from 7 pm and the shows begin an hour or so later.

Away from the center of the city is the **Villa Saujana** on Jalan Loyang. Its vast gardens are the setting for a buffet dinner of Malay food, drinks and local fresh fruits for dessert. For entertainment guests are treated to Malay, Chinese and Indian folk dances. This dinner is bookable through local tour operators.

For dining and dancing, usually with entertainment laid on, there's **The Tiara** on the 25th floor of the Shangri-La (phone ahead for reservations and showtimes); the **Kasbah** on the 36th floor or the **Belvedere** at the Mandarin; the **West End Club** at the Goodwood Park. There's also dancing by the rooftop pool of the Singapore Hilton where you can have drinks and a barbecue dinner at the **Tradewinds**. Be prepared for strong breezes up there. Some places may specify that you spend a minimum amount on your food; others may slap on a cover charge. A dinner-theater or dinner-concert may come with the package for the evening. Check dress requirements when going to the smart places in town. Some may require a tie for men or national dress.

Theater-restaurants offering floor shows or international entertainment, live bands and songstresses along with Chinese dinner include the **Orchid Lantern Theatre Restaurant**; **Golden Million** at the Peninsula Hotel (seating 1000); **The Raja** at the Great Eastern Hotel; the **Silver Star** at the Orchard Building on Grange Road. The **Neptune Theatre Restaurant** at the Overseas Union House in Collyer Quay (seating 1200, reputedly the biggest in Southeast Asia) offers a Chinese dinner with a variety show consisting of cultural dances, modern dances and a magic show. If you wish to join a night tour featuring dinner in a theater-restaurant, enquire from the tour desk at your hotel.

Cabarets, with dance hostesses (at S$15 an hour; arrangements are made with "captains") include the **Apollo** at the Apollo Hotel, **Oasis** at Kallang Park, **Multi-storey Car Park Night Club**, and **Maxim's** at Supreme House on Penang Road (a day and night cabaret). There may be a cover charge under S$5. These cabarets feature local and foreign entertainers.

Dinner Cruise

For something different, you could sign up for a dinner cruise aboard a Chinese junk. Built of ironwood, these former "workhorses" of the seas had colorful histories. With their billowing sails, they carried cargoes of copra, rubber, coal and timber. Modern bridges and flyovers have forced them to dismantle their sails and saw off their masts, and install engines instead. Such is the junk of the East Wind.

As you pull away from the pier, you see the city's skyline receding
and the figure of the Merlion spewing water from its mouth. Then you
go past the ships lying at anchor and lighters carrying cargo to and from
shore. The junk skirts the southern islands of Pulau Brani, Kusu, Pulau
Terkukor, goes around Sentosa and along the coastline of Singapore's
mainland, and **Keppel Harbour**. The cruise, with a buffet dinner on
board, takes about three hours. Starting time is 6 pm from the Clifford
Pier. Carry a light cardigan if you are susceptible to colds as it can get
windy. Dinner cruises are operated by East Wind and Watertours; prices
range from S$30 and S$36, half price for children below 12. Again, it is
best to call the companies to find out the price as this is likely to change.

Chinatown at Night

Trishaw tours are promoted as a way of seeing Chinatown at night.
The tour takes an hour or two and usually starts from Raffles Hotel, but
it could be on Orchard Road too.

Establish fares before boarding the trishaw. Usually it costs S$32 for
a tour which may conclude with a Singapore Gin Sling at the historic
Raffles Hotel, but you may be able to bargain this down if you wish to
have a shorter tour. Your driver pedals along the wide avenues of the
business district where modern skyscrapers look down on 19th-century
weather-worn two-story buildings. The swoosh of vehicular traffic
beside the frail buggy is not calculated to ease the mind or allay the fears
of the faint-hearted.

The **night markets** of Chinatown are alive with diners and shoppers
and pedestrians. Naked light bulbs glow brightly from makeshift stalls
festooned with all manner of merchandise, from dried meat to clothes,
umbrellas, bags and fancy goods. Fruits are piled in colorful array,
sweets and artificial flowers are displayed in gay abandon. Small tables
fill up with customers as hawkers prepare steaming bowls of noodles
and other delicacies from the food stalls nearby. There is a constant
stream of people on the street and the trishaw driver is hard put not to
run over anyone, particularly as most of the pedestrians seem oblivious
of the frantic tooting of the horn. It's all good fun for those who like that
sort of thing.

Festivals

Festivals are bright flecks in the fabric of life and in Singapore the
flecks are many and varied. For every month of the year there is a
festival going on, whether it is to greet a new year, to celebrate a deity's
birthday, to commemorate the death of a martyr, to appease hungry
ghosts, to mark the end of a month-long fast, to rejoice at the fullness of
the moon, or to honor deities of one kind or another.

If you can, time your visit to coincide with one of the major festivals
as this is an excellent way of appreciating the multiracial culture of
Singapore. Buddhists, Taoists, Christians, Hindus and Moslems have
their own festivals and celebrations at various times of the year. Most of
these are movable feasts, depending on what calendar is used to reckon
time.

At such festivals you may hear the beating of drums and gongs, the
clashing of cymbals or the chanting of prayers and singing of hymns;
you may be treated to a spectacular display of fireworks or a colorful
procession or parade; you may see joss sticks and candles lighted in
temples and altars, bonfires of paper houses, paper cars and spirit
money. You may taste specially prepared delicacies. All these impart a
distinct flavor to your stay.

Because some festivals are lunar festivals, the dates are not fixed.
Chinese New Year, for example, may occur in the month of January one
year, February the next. The Moslem feast of Hari Raya Puasa or the start
of Ramadan, the Thai water festival, the Hindu festival of lights, the
dragon boat and mid-autumn festivals of the Chinese, are all reckoned
by different calendars and so do not fall on the same date from year to
year. The variation, however, occurs within a period of not more than
two months.

It is important to note certain local customs and rules of conduct
when visiting places of worship. In a Hindu temple or Moslem mosque
shoes are taken off at the entrance. Women are not allowed in the main
hall during important Moslem festivities. Their place is at the upper
gallery, which is somewhat like a choir loft. A woman is not supposed to
enter a mosque or Hindu temple when she has her menses (the
connotation being that she is unclean during this period). Although
visitors are permitted to take photographs during ceremonies, they
should not make a nuisance of themselves by clambering onto windows,
perching on church pews, or entering areas reserved only for priests and
their attendants. Conservative dress for women is called for (no mini
skirts or short shorts; sometimes even pants are not permitted if the
mosque is ultra conservative).

The New Year (January 1) is ushered in by the sounding of ship's
bells from the harbor. In nightclubs and hotels gala dinners and balls and
special shows are organized to bring in the new year.

Lunar New Year (January or February) – Before the old year ends,
people are busy sprucing up their homes. This annual house-cleaning is
equivalent to the spring cleaning in Western countries. Housewives
stock up on food provisions; new clothes are bought to be worn in the
new year and debts are paid off. Calligraphers do a brisk trade writing
felicitous messages on red scrolls which are pasted on doorways or hung
inside the house. Flower fairs spring up, selling peach blossoms,

Roadside food stalls along Bugis Street.

symbolic of longevity, narcissus, pussywillows and golden kumquats, all symbols of good fortune and prosperity.

Traditional Chinese families hold their grand reunion. It is customary to eat a fish dish, fish being considered propitious. Children and young unmarried people receive red packets of lucky money called *ang pow* in Singapore (in Hong Kong it is known as *lai see*). Sweeping the house is forbidden as this could mean sweeping away luck. On the first two days of the new year, people are not supposed to work, hence many Chinese shops and restaurants are closed on these days. The celebration lasts for fifteen days.

Ponggol (January) – This is a harvest festival celebrated in the southern part of India and brought to Singapore by the Tamils. Dedicated to the Sun God, it is held in the second week of January. In homes and temples, the festival is marked with thanksgiving prayers and offerings of rice, vegetable curry, spices and sugar cane.

Rice is cooked in the morning in a new and shining pot. The water is allowed to boil over, signifying an excess of prosperity. Rice is again cooked ceremoniously in temples in the evenings. The cooked rice is laid out on banana leaves and, together with other vegetarian dishes, offered for blessing. The consecrated food, known as *prasadam,* is distributed. It is believed that those who partake of this sacred food are cleansed of their sins.

Visitors who wish to see the temple rites during the four-day festival should go to the Perumal Temple on Serangoon Road (also known as "Little India"). The beating of drums, chiming of bells and blowing of Indian conch shells accompanies the singing of hymns. Ponggol greeting cards showing a maiden carrying an earthern vessel overflowing with rice are sold in the Indian shops in the area.

Maulidin Nabi (December or January) – The birthday of the prophet Mohammed on the twelfth day of the third month of the Moslem calendar is a day of prayers and sermons for Moslems. Chanting the "Murhaban", they extol the works and achievements of the prophet. At seven in the evening all mosques in Singapore hold a recital of the *Berjanzi,* a book of the life of Mohammed. The Sultan Mosque on North Bridge Road (10 minutes by taxi from the hotels in the vicinity of Orchard Road, see p.97) has the biggest celebration.

Thaipusam (January – This is a Hindu festival commemorating the victory of Lord Subramaniam, a popular Hindu god, over Idumban, the demon. The bedecked image of the deity is borne in procession on a lighted chariot from the Chettiar Temple on Tank Road through the streets of the city, stopping at the Sri Mariamman Temple in Chinatown where the deity's mother is housed, and ending at the Vinayakar Temple, where the deity remains until evening. On the way back, Lord Subramaniam is carried past the business houses of the Chettiars or money lenders at Market Street, to acknowledge their financial support of his temple.

The other part of the festival is the procession of the kavadi-bearers. the *kavadi* is either a metal or a wooden arch decorated with feathers and flowers and studded with sharp spikes, borne on the shoulders of men as a form of penance or in fulfillment of a pledge. Some may regard the carrying of the kavadi as a barbaric rite, and in India the practice is banned. But it flourishes in Singapore and Malaysia.

Weeks before the festival, the kavadi-bearers abstain from eating meat and drinking alcoholic beverages. On the morning of the procession they have a purifying bath and by means of chants put themselves into a hypnotic trance. In this state, they pierce their body, arms and face with skewers and fishhooks from which hang such objects as fruits, coconuts, and metal ornaments. then they take up the kavadi.

The bizarre procession begins at the Perumal Temple on Serangoon Road to the cheers of thousands of onlookers who encourage the kavadi-bearers with shouts of "Vel! Vel!"; passes through Orchard Road and Clemenceau Avenue. At two temples en route, coconuts are broken and offered to the gods. The procession winds up at the Chettiar Temple where the devotees pour milk over the image of the Lord Subramaniam and in turn receive food and milk. The ceremony ends when the kavadis and skewers are removed from the bodies of the participants who rub themselves with a kind of powder. Strangely the skewers and spikes leave no marks or scars.

Chingay (January or February) – Chingay means a decorated float. The term comes from the fact that in China in the olden days floats were carried on the shoulders of men during the Lunar New Year to honor their tutelary deities and gods. The celebration is usually held on the first weekend following Chinese New Year. In Singapore, Chingay is basically still a Chinese tradition, featuring lion and dragon dances. But it has evolved into a spectacular national parade. A giant flag is carried by a team displaying their collective and individual skills; acrobats and martial artists show their prowess by performing daring acts like leaping over sharp swords and spears. Over the years tableaux showing fairy tale characters and the various national groups that make up Singapore's polyglot population have been added. Thus there are Indian dancers and stilt-walkers, a tableau of a Malay wedding, Snow White and the Seven Dwarfs, Alice in Wonderland, pom pom girls and school bands, roller skaters, warriors and swordsmen, and military bands.

Monkey God's Birthday – In legend, the Monkey God began life as the king of the monkeys. He wanted to live forever so he stole and ate a peach of immortality from heaven. Full of tricks, he can change himself into any one of 72 forms (Chinese consider the figure 72 synonymous with eternity), control the tide with the wave of a magic rod (which he stole) and somersault 108,000 leagues. The monkey figures prominently in the Chinese tale *Journey to the West* in which a monk (Hsuan Tsang) journeyed to India to learn the precepts of Buddha which he brought

back to China. In the journey, the monk, the monkey and the pig encountered many difficulties but the wiles and agility of the monkey saved them. For this he was made a god, and granted the title "Great Sage Equal to Heaven".

The Monkey God's birthday is celebrated twice a year (in February or March and again in September or October) in various Chinese temples, but mainly at Eng Hoon Street and Cumming Street. Altars housing the Monkey God and other heavenly deities are constructed. The ceremonies are performed by mediums, said to be possessed by the spirit of the Monkey God. Although they inflict wounds on themselves, not a drop of blood is spilt, and no pain felt.

On the eve of the birthday, one medium dips himself in water strewn with flowers of many hues. He is then led to a red "dragon chair" and dressed in the robes of the Monkey God. Suddenly, he leaps about, scribbles figures on pieces of paper which fortune-hunters try hard to decipher as they are thought to be the winning numbers in the next lottery, and cracks the whip over the shoulders of the devotees, giving each a paper charm. The ceremony lasts for three hours.

The following day, more mediums dressed in Monkey God attire go into a trance. Spears pierce their cheeks and holy paper is stuffed into their mouths. They lead a procession which includes a sedan chair bearing the image of the god. In the meantime, Chinese operas and puppet shows are performed in the temple grounds. At the end of the ceremony, a paper palace is burnt to honor the deity.

Birthday of the Saint of the Poor – To mark the birthday of the saint of the poor – Kong Teck Choon Ong – in March, a grand street parade is held. Mediums go into a trance, pierce their cheeks, arms and tongues with skewers and carry on their shoulders a decorated palanquin bearing the saint's image. The center of the celebration is the White Cloud Temple on Ganges Ave. Mediums from other temples join in the procession and as the palanquin passes, spectators show their reverence by pressing their hands together.

Ching Ming (April) – The dead are remembered by the living on this day (a movable date, usually in April). Chinese families, armed with shears, shovels and lawnmowers, clean the graves of their ancestors and lay offerings of food and flowers. A festive atmosphere prevails as people picnic on grave sites. In the homes, willow branches are hung over doorways to prevent evil spirits from entering.

Good Friday (March or April) – Christian churches commemorate Christ's death on the cross with solemn services, among which is a candlelight procession bearing the figure of Christ in the grounds of the Church of St. Joseph on Victoria Street.

Songkran Festival (April) – Celebrated in Thai Buddhist temples, Songkran ushers in the new year. The image of Buddha is bathed with

The faithful of Islam pray at the Sultan Mosque.

perfumed holy water. The center of celebration are the Ananda Metyarama Thai Buddhist Temple on Silat Road and Sapthapuchaniyaram Temple on Holland Road. Be prepared to get wet as part of the festival involves throwing water at other people. Water is poured on elders and monks as a sign of veneration. There is folk dancing and religious music.

Birthday of the Third Prince (May) – The Third Prince of the Lotus, depicted with one hand holding a magic spear and the other a magic bracelet, is a child god who is worshipped as a hero and a miracle-worker. Pantomimes and street operas are performed on a stage set up near the temple dedicated in his honor. This is located at the corner of Clarke Street and North Boat Quay, close to Chinatown. The performance starts at noon. In the evening, the temple mediums go into a trance, cut themselves with swords and spikes and with their blood write charms on strips of paper which are much sought after by their followers. Paper replicas of houses, palaces and cars are burnt as an offering to the gods. Then to the accompaniment of drums, gongs and wind instruments, a procession of floats, stilt-walkers, dragon and lion dancers winds its way along the streets.

Vesak Day (May) – Sacred to Buddhists throughout the world, the day commemorates the birth anniversary, enlightenment and the entry of the Buddha into Nirvana. The celebration is held on the full moon during the month of Visakha. Homes are decked with religious flags and temples glow with myriad lights. Devout Buddhists visit temples to attend services, to pray and meditate, to see relics of the Buddha and make donations to the monks. Temple ceremonies start as early as 6.30 am with monks chanting sutras. Candlelight processions led by flower girls bearing urns which hold relics of the Buddha are held in the evening.

This is a day for giving to charity and for being kind to beggars and animals by giving them food. Caged birds are released on this day as the Buddhists believe that they gained merit in the eyes of the Buddha by so doing. Temple ceremonies are held at the Theravada Buddhist Temple on 30-C St Michael's Road; the Temple of 1000 Lights on Race Course Road, just 15 minutes away by taxi from Orchard Road, the Mangala Vihara Buddhist Temple at Jalan Eunos, and Pher Kark See on Bright Hill Drive.

Dragon Boat Festival (June) – The festival commemorates the death of a Chinese poet and state official who drowned himself in the river to protest against the injustice and corruption of his time. Fishermen, commiserating his death, threw dumplings into the water to prevent fish from eating the body. Thus was born the practice of preparing *chang*, which are eaten at home or presented to friends and relatives. *Changs* are dumplings made of glutinous rice with a filling of spiced meat, salted egg yolks and bean paste, which are wrapped in bamboo leaves and then steamed. Sometimes the dumplings have no filling and are eaten with sugar or syrup.

A feature of the festival is the holding of the dragon and phoenix boat races. Only men are allowed by tradition to row dragon boats; to show that there is no discrimination of the sexes, phoenix boat races were introduced so that women could take part in the festival.

Ramadan (July) – The month-long fast of Moslems start on the first day of the ninth month of the Islamic calendar (sometime in July). All Moslems are required by their religion to forgo all food and drink, including water, for 30 days during the daylight hours. The daily fast is broken at sundown when the sacred cannon sounds. After their meal, the men go to the mosque to pray.

Along Arab Street and the vicinity of the Sultan Mosque food stalls spring up selling various kinds of delicacies loved by Malays and Indians – rice cakes wrapped in banana leaves; custards flavored with syrup; roasted coconut flakes and other goodies, in anticipation of the devout who will soon break their fast. This is a good opportunity if you are in town during Ramadan to sample some dishes which are seldom seen at any other time.

Hari Raya Puasa (August) – The first day of the tenth moon in the Moslem calendar is a time for celebration, signaling the end of Ramadan. It begins with the sighting of the new moon. In the morning thanksgiving prayers are conducted in the mosques, followed by feasting and visits to friends and relatives.

Days before the occasion, women shop for new clothes to be worn during the festival and prepare the household for the feasting. Each house vies in the grandeur of its preparation. The woman of the house turns out as many sweets and delicacies as she is capable of and these are served in huge platters by the children to the guests.

Hungry Ghosts Festival (August) – Traditionally held on the seventh moon, this is a time when disembodied spirits or ghosts are released from the underworld and for one month are free to roam about among the living. These are restless spirits who may have died without proper burial ceremonies, or have no progeny to remember them during Ching Ming or Chung Yeung. Hence they must be appeased by the living or they may do great harm.

To placate them, sticks of incense, paper money, houses, clothing, cars, etc. are burnt, food is offered and Chinese street operas are performed for their entertainment. In keeping with the modern times, some organizers of the community festivities even hold pop concerts! These ceremonies and events take place in marketplaces and temples, and on street corners. The celebration of this festival in Singapore is noisy and colorful.

The climax is the holding of a feast in which a dining table is lavishly laid with food. Three officiating deities are present at the feast – the God of Longevity, the Goddess of Mercy and Da Shi Ye, Inspector of the Homeless Ghosts. A huge papier-mâché figure of Da Shi Ye presides

TEXTILE CENTRE

SULTAN PLAZA
PLAZA BOWL
TOON HIN PAWN-SHOP
ASHON TEXTILES
BARAKATH

at the head of the table. The empty chairs next to him are reserved for the two gods. Under his stern eye, Da Shi Ye sees to it that all the ghosts have their share of the feast. Later the organizers share the food and take it home.

In Singapore, the living also have their own feasts – Chinese banquets at which auctions are held to raise funds for the next festival. People bid for such items as potted plants and flowers, ceramic statues of deities, household items. The most popular of the items up for auction is the "Black gold", a ceremonial piece of charcoal which is believed to contain all the powers of the spirits attending the feasts. Bidders have been known to pay as much as S$20,000 for a piece. No money passes hands at these auctions as payments are made when needed during the next festival. Of course no one has ever reneged on his promise as the creditors belong to the spirit world.

On the last day of the month-long festival, traditional Chinese stay at home as this is the time when the ghosts are hurrying back to the underworld before the gates close on them. Woe to the person who is caught by a stray spirit. The Chinese believe that this person may not live through another year.

Mooncake Festival (September or October) – Celebrated on the 15th day of the eighth moon, the one night in the year when the moon is at its roundest and brightest, so the Chinese believe. There are competitions to create the best lanterns. It is the custom for children to carry lighted lanterns in processions throughout the island. An integral part of the festival is the eating of mooncakes, a rich concoction of bean paste with melon or lotus seeds in a round crust of pastry. The more expensive contain an addition orange peel, spices and egg yolks.

There is no consensus as to the exact origin of the festival. Some claim that it commemorates the victory of Chinese patriots who overthrew the Mongols during the Ming Dynasty. Messages were hidden inside mooncakes and lanterns were used to signal the start of the rebellion.

Another story tells of a tyrannical king who found the drink of immortality but whose wife, concerned for his subjects, decided to destroy it. She was caught in the act, however. To avoid certain punishment, she swallowed the elixir and leaped to make her escape. The leap landed her on the moon where she now dwells. Each year during the Moon Festival, people gaze at the moon to catch a glimpse of her image.

Double Ninth (October) – The ninth day of the ninth moon in the Chinese calendar is an auspicious day. On this day people take to the hills or climb heights and clean the graves (usually located on hillsides) of their ancestors.

The origin of the custom of going to mountains or hills dates back to the Han Dynasty (206 BC to 220 AD) when a man named Huan Ching

(preceding page) Sultan Mosque, Singapore's largest mosque.

was advised by a sage to flee to the mountains with his wife and family on the ninth day of the ninth moon to escape from disaster. Returning home the following day, the man found all the animals on his farm dead.

Nine Emperor Gods (September or October) – The first nine days of the ninth moon are dedicated to the Nine Chinese Emperors who have been deified. These Emperor Gods are said to cure ailments, grant long life and shower good luck. In the temple of Upper Serangoon Road and at Lorong Tai Seng, close to the old Paya Lebar Airport, mediums go into a trance and during the evening procession escort the decorated sedan chairs bearing the images of the gods.

Hari Raya Haji (October) – This is the Moslem festival pilgrimage. Moslems rise early, bathe, and put on new clothes before going to the mosque where they prostrate themselves in prayer and listen to sermons and speeches. This is a time for forgiveness; a time to patch up quarrels and renew friendships; a time for alms-giving and for remembering the poor.

Thimithi Festival (October) – This festival, which entails walking over burning coals, honors the purity of the Goddess Durobatha or Droba Devi. According to the Hindu epic, *Mahabharata*, Durobatha was taken as a booty by Prince Arjuna when he vanquished Durobatha's father in battle. Arjuna's mother decreed that Durobatha should be shared by Arjuna's four brothers and that she should stay with each brother for a period of one year. Durobatha did as she was ordered but to prove her purity, she walked on burning embers. Hindus believe that only the pure in mind and soul can escape fire unscathed.

During the festival, the devout pray to the goddess for help. Those whose prayers have been granted walk on burning coals in gratitude for the favor given them. Days before the festival, the supplicants prepare themselves by fasting and prayer. Then on the day of the festival a pit seven meters (23 ft) wide is filled with firewood and set alight. Amid prayers and chantings, the devotees step on the burning coals barefoot.

The Sri Mariamman Temple on South Bridge Road is a good place to watch the festival in progress. Those who arrive early will witness the ritual baths of the supplicants and the whip-lashings inflicted upon them as a means of penance by the priests. Some fire-walkers dash across the pit, but most attempt to walk serenely across the glowing embers.

Navarathi Festival – This is the homage to the Hindu trinity, lasting ten days and nine nights. Prayers, hymns and classical dances are held in the Hindu temples while in private homes, the images of the gods and goddesses are displayed in the best room, together with a beautifully dressed retinue of dolls.

The first three days are dedicated to the worship of the Goddess Durga, also known as Parvathi, consort of Lord Siva the Destroyer. In various Hindu temples her statue is laden with flower garlands and offerings are laid at her feet. The next three days are for the veneration of Lakshmi, Goddess of Wealth and consort of Lord Vishnu the Protector.

The last three days are dedicated to Saraswathi, Goddess of Education, Literature, Music and Eloquence, and consort of Lord Brahma the Creator. Worshipers lay books and musical instruments before her statue. Among the traditional Hindus the tenth day is when a learned man, or *pandit*, is invited to their homes to begin the formal education of their children. The young ones are taught to write Om, the universal word, and Hari, which means Vishnu.

At the Chettiar Temple on Tank Road, visitors can see classical Indian dances to the accompaniment of music from traditional Indian instruments, every evening between seven and ten o'clock during the nine nights of the festival. The last two days of the festival are spent in feasting and merrymaking.

The climax is a grand evening procession with the statue of a silver horse as the focal point. Women resplendent in their saris follow the image in a procession that winds through River Valley Road, Killiney Road, Orchard Road and Clemenceau Avenue before returning to the Chettiar Temple.

Deepavali Festival (October or November) – This Hindu festival of lights is one of the most important in the Hindu calendar. According to some sources the festival celebrates the victory of Lord Krishna over the demon king Nasakasura. Others suggests that this is one day in the year when the goddess Lakshmi visits the earth. Whatever the origin of the festival, it is universally celebrated by Hindus who prepare for the festival by thoroughly cleaning their homes and praying for departed members of the family whose souls are believed to return to earth at this time. Members of the family gather to pray for the souls of their departed and food is offered in front of photographs of their dead loved ones.

One the eve of the festival, rows of oil lamps (*Deepavali* means a row of lights), colored lamps and candles are lighted and members of the family, who have donned new clothes, sit up all night with all doors and windows open, to welcome the goddess Lakshmi.

Visitors who are in Singapore at this time will see Hindu temples all lighted up, with abundant offerings of fruits and flowers placed before the shrines. In the evening a grand procession is held, bearing the image of the temple's presiding deity. The Perumal Temple on Serangoon Road in Little India is one of the best places to watch this festival.

Christmas (December) – All the accouterments of Christmas in the West can be seen in Singapore – Christmas trees, lights, Santa Claus and his sleigh pulled by reindeer, decorated malls and shop windows and carolers singing Christmas carols. Special menus are prepared by hotels and stores hold big Christmas sales. On Christmas Eve, radio and television stations broadcast special shows, and midnight masses are held in Catholic churches. Christmas Day services are also held in the Christian churches.

The Buddhist Siong Lim Temple.

王殿
雙林寺
景敷互重瀛西土宗風終不墜
萬山滌盪鏡帶逍迴
一水心樹色參院蘭若禪
無事波洺梓沽鈿馬

Food and Drink

The entrepôt character of Singapore with its mixture of races and ethnic groups has give rise to a cuisine rich in variety and nuance. Chinese, Indian, Malay, Western and Nonya – all contribute to give you an exciting taste treat, a gourmet's repast. You can have a feast in food hawker's stall by the roadside or at any of the vast food centers that have sprung up in recent years, in a restaurant decorated to look like a palace or in an elegant candlelit hotel dining room. There are also fast food shops offering inexpensive meals, coffee houses and pubs.

The astonishing number and variety of eating places present a pleasant dilemma to someone who wants to sample good Singaporean food. The only guidelines are your personal preferences – whether you wish to eat Chinese, Indian, Malay, Nonya, or Western food, and whether you have the urge to splurge and eat in style or you are on a budget.

Unless you have a tight itinerary where your meals are all accounted for, or you have business luncheons lined up, you can take advantage of the lunch hour to sample the eating places in the area where you are browsing, sightseeing or shopping.

Chinese

Many visitors are familiar with Chinese food and in Singapore you will find an extensive choice ranging from the dishes of the south (Cantonese, Hainanese, Hakka and Teochew) to those of the north (Beijing and Hunanese) with Fukienese, Shanghainese, Sichuan and Yunnan in between.

Western palates are perhaps most familiar with Cantonese cuisine, with its roast duck and goose, suckling pig, shark's fin soup, and *dim sum*. Some of the restaurants serving good Cantonese fare are: **Chinese Inn** (G42-47 Lucky Plaza), an inexpensive restaurant suitable for lunch or a light dinner. Their specialities are congee (rice porridge) and noodles served with prawns, pork, kidney, fish, tripe or liver; **Fatty's (Win Seong) Restaurant** (184 Albert Street), popular with locals and tourists, inexpensive and not air-conditioned. It has good spring rolls, sweet and sour pork, crab claws and roast chicken. **Mayflower Restaurant** (DBS Building, Shenton Way or the Peking Mayflower at the International Building, Orchard Road), open for lunch and dinner, offers good dim sum during lunchtime, and is also known for its roast duck, shark's fin soup and suckling pig. On the expensive side. The **Shang Palace** at Shangri-la Hotel also specializes in dim sum lunches and à la carte dinners. Their roast duck, bird's nest soup, abalone, beef steaks, crystal prawns and barbecued chicken are recommended. Expensive.

Teochew food is well-known for sliced salted goose meat eaten cold, oysters in salty fermented black bean sauce, abalone with sautéd spinach, salted vegetable and duck soup, steamed pomfret, sea cucumber and prawn rolls and fish porridge. Good Teochew restaurants are **Swatow Teochew Restaurant** (1st floor, Singapore Conference Hall, Shenton Way or Podium B15 Basement of the DBS Building, Shenton Way), **Guan Hin** (1 Bendemeer Road, corner Whampoa West) and **Ban Seng Restaurant** (79 New Bridge Road).

Hakka food, like Teochew, is mild. Best known of the dishes are the bean curd, brinjals and bitter gourd stuffed with fish paste and cooked with fish balls (*niang dou fu*), and stewed duck with sea cucumber. Hainan is known for its steamed rice topped with chicken chunks and flavored with oil and ginger and "steamboat" meals, highly popular in Singapore. **Swee Kee Chicken Rice Restaurant** (51/53 Middle Road) specializes in steamed chicken rice and is very inexpensive. Try the Hainan roast pork and chicken rice at **Yet Con Restaurant** (25 Purvis Street). Another good Hakka restaurant is **Moi Kong** (22 Murray Street, Food Alley, off Maxwell Road).

Of the Beijing dishes, the most well known is Beijing duck, the succulently crisp skin encased in a dumpling wrapper, garnished with green onions and sliced cucumber and eaten with a plum sauce. **Eastern Palace** (4th floor, Supreme House) serves banquet fare in an elegant setting. Quite expensive. **Pine Court** (36th floor, Mandarin Hotel) also specializes in Peking duck, fresh water fish from China served with a sweet vinegar-soy gravy. The setting is elegant and the price of a meal expensive.

Spiced and honeyed baked ham is a Hunanese speciality, as is minced pigeon in bamboo cup, stewed mutton webs and sliced fish in chicken soup. Hunanese use a lot of sauces usually prepared with plenty of garlic, brown sugar, ginger and vinegar. A good place to have Hunanese food is at the **Apollo Theatre Restaurant and Nightclub** (Apollo Hotel, Havelock Rd).

Sichuan food is characterized by its use of chillis and peppers. Smoked duck Sichuan style, prawns fried with dried chilli, sweet and sour soup, sautéed eggplant with minced pork and chilli, and fried shredded eels in rich garlic sauce are among the most popular of the dishes. **Golden Phoenix** (2nd floor, Hotel Equatorial), **Omei** (Hotel Grand Central) and Meisan Szechuan Restaurant (2nd floor Holiday Inn), all have good Sichuan food. Most dishes are accompanied by roast or steamed buns and finished off with a sweet red bean pancake.

Shanghainese dishes include drunken chicken (wine-soused chicken), braised meat balls, braised eels and vegetables such as cabbage or lettuce served with a creamy sauce.

Hokkien or Fujian food is prepared with cloves, soy sauce, cinnamon and sometimes garlic. Hokkien *mee* noodles are great favorites, as well as stewed pork in black sauce, spring rolls known as *bao bing* and a sandwich-type bun filled with stewed pork in black sauce.

(above) Fresh seafood, sold in the open markets.
(opposite page) Serangoon Road's cooks prepare traditional Indian dishes.

A good Hokkien restaurant is **Beng Thin Hoon Kee Restaurant** (4th floor, OCBC Centre, 65 Chulia Street). Prices are reasonable.

Southern Chinese are rice-eaters while the coastal and northern inhabitants prefer buns and noodles made of wheat.

Indian

There are two main divisions of Indian cooking: northern and southern. (The latter is further subdivided into Hindu and Moslem.) Curry cuts across boundaries, but the southern curries are more fiery than the northern which are milder yet lack none of the flavor. The curry is served with liberal helpings of steamed rice, chutney sauces and condiments which may include spicy grated coconut, pickled sour lemon rinds and sweet mangoes. Also popular is *dal*, a lentil porridge.

An Indian vegetarian meal may consist of five or six curries, rice, *papadam* (the crisp thin bread and chutney served with *tairu* (yoghurt) and *rasam* (pepper water).

Among the well-known northern Indian dishes are chicken tandoori – chicken marinated in a mixture of yoghurt, lime, lemon and spices and baked slowly in a clay oven (*tandoor*) – and shish kebab, cubes of mutton cooked on skewers. Typically southern dishes are *dosai* (a type of pancake), mutton and fish curry. Dosai is a favorite of vegetarians. A plain pancake is called *mau dosai*. Filled with peas, carrots and potatoes it

is a *masala dosai*; stuffed with onion it is *venegayah dosai*. When the batter is made from wholemeal flour it is *rava dosai*. Other Indian breads are the crisp and thin *papad* or *papadam*, made from bean flour paste; the *naan*, another type of plain pancake; the *prata*, dough spread into a thin film about a meter wide, then folded and fried slowly on a very large griddle. (When filled with minced meat, onion and egg, it becomes *murtabak*.) the *prata* and the *murtabak* are eaten with any type of curry.

Other popular Indian dishes are *rojak*, a selection of various ingredients such as fried bean curd, cuttlefish, eggs, potatoes, prawn fritters and lettuce dipped into a slightly hot and sweet sauce; *mee goreng* – fried noodles garnished with cabbage strips, eggs, tomatoes,sauce, peas and mutton; *kambing soup* – spicy mutton soup eaten with French bread; *nasi biryani* – saffron rice mixed with pieces of mutton or chicken.

Among the restaurants serving Northern Indian food are **Omar Khayyam** (55 Hill Street, fairly expensive), **Rang Mahal** (Oberoi-Imperial Hotel), and **Shalimar** (4th floor, Tanglin Shopping Centre, Tanglin Road. The Southern Indian restaurants are **Jubille** (771 North Bridge Road, near Arab Street), **Muthu's Curry Restaurant** (78 Race Course Road), and **Race Course Restaurant** (36 Race Course Road). Try the fish head curry at these two places.

Malay

Malay food is hot and spicy, made so by the liberal use of spices and condiments such as chilli, cloves, coriander, tamarind and coconut milk. *Satay* is the best-known of the Malay dishes. Pieces of beef or chicken are marinated and threaded in skewers and then broiled over a charcoal fire. It is served with cucumber chunks and onions. Dipped in a sauce blended from coconut milk, ground nuts and spices with a dash of chilli, it is eaten with *ketupat* – cooked rice wrapped in coconut leaves. Other Malay specialities are *mee rebus* (noodles cooked in a spicy sauce and eaten with a squeeze of lime juice), *lontong* – rice cake in vegetable curry sauce; beef *rendang*, fried anchovies, *tempeh* (beancurd cake), curried eggs and fried fish.

Aziza (36 Emerald Hill Road) is a Western-style restaurant serving Malay cuisine at reasonable prices. Specialties are *tari* (beef) *rendang*, *oporan* chicken, squid stuffed with fresh tomatoes and fried in spices and *kangkong* (local spinach) fried with prawn pasta and fresh chilli. **Nasi Padang** (24 Tanglin Road) and **Rendezvous** (4-5 Bras Basah Road) also serve good Malay food.

Peranakan or Nonya

The Straits-born Chinese, inhabitants and descendants of the former Straits Settlements (Singapore, Penang and Malacca), have developed a distinct cuisine which is a combination of the Chinese and Malay styles of cooking. This has come to be known as Nonya or Peranakan cooking.

The mixture of Chinese, Malay and Indonesian ingredients make for an interesting taste.

Like typical Malay and Indonesian fare, Nonya cooking uses seasonings such as garlic, turmeric, ginger, cumin, coriander, chilli, spring onions, lemon grass and candlenuts. The result is hot and spicy. Unlike Malay and Indonesian food, however, Nonya dishes use pork. Some of the famous Nonya dishes are chicken *lemak* (chicken cooked in coconut milk), *laksa* (thin rice noodles cooked in coconut milk and spices and garnished with prawns, bean sprouts and sliced fish balls), *lontong*, and *mee siam* (rice vermicelli in a tangy sauce served with bean sprouts and slices of boiled egg; can be eaten with or without chilli).

Wen's Place (formerly Chrisvic Corner, 101-A, Block 4, Queen's Road) is known for its *Penang Laksa, Ikan Asam Padas* or hot sour fish cooked in coconut cream, spicy beef, and *ayam buah keluak* (chicken in chilli sauce). The **Apollo** Hotel's Coffee Shop also offers a buffet luncheon of Nonya dishes.

Other Asian Restaurants

Indonesian food, hot and spicy like Malay food but slightly sweeter, is readily found in Singapore. *Gado-gado*, a vegetable salad with peanut sauce, and satay are popular. **The Metro Indonesian Restaurant** (1st floor, Metro Golden Mile, Merlin Plaza) is a good place to try Indonesian food. *Soto ayam, laksa lemak* and *Ikan asam* are specialties.

Korean restaurants include **Ham-Po Korean Restaurant** (3rd floor, Mohan Shopping Centre, 321 Orchard Road) which specializes in *bulgogi* barbecued meat cooked on the table and served with side dishes such as *kin chi* (pickled and spicy cabbage, radish, and cucumber slices), cuttlefish fried in hot and sweet sauce, raw fish and a beancurd stew, and the **Korean Restaurant** (4th floor, Specialists' Shopping Centre, Orchard Road) which also features *bulgogi*.

Among the Japanese restaurants are the **Singapore Okoh Japanese Restaurant** (4th floor, Supreme House) which, in addition to *tepanyaki, sukiyaki* and *sushi*, is famous for its fixed price buffet barbecue dinners. You can take all you want but you pay a penalty for leftovers by getting charged extra for them. Then there is **Kanako** (7-12 Parklane Arcade, Goodwood Park Hotel), small but expensive, and **Mino-Q** (1st floor, King's Hotel, Havelock Road) which has good food, good service and a nice decor; **Kampachi Japanese Restaurant** (Hotel Equatorial, 429 Bukit Timah Road and the Japanese restaurants in the Mandarin Hotel, Hotel Miramar, York Hotel, Century Park Sheraton, Apollo Singapore and Hotel Royal.

Hawker Centers

If you want to eat as the natives do, then point your nose to where the local food is best – in hawker stalls and food complexes. There is a high degree of sanitation in hawker centers so unless you have a very

(above) A flower market at the junction of Emerald Hill Road.
(oppsoite page) Selecting the best chillis from the open market, Chinatown.

frail stomach you should be able to enjoy your food without any
untoward consequences.

Hawker centers offer a wide variety of local food: Chinese, Indian,
Malay, Nonya. Home-style cooking handed down from generation to
generation is the proud heritage of some of the hawker stalls whose
cooks carry the culinary secrets of their forebears. Some of these food
stalls have acquired a faithful clientele over the years. Their patrons do
not mind traveling a great distance just to eat their favorite food from
these stalls.

What to order: Eat as the Singaporeans eat. Noodles come in a
variety of preparations, from mild to spicy. Try: *Hokkien mee* – yellow
wheat noodles garnished with prawns and bean sprouts; fishball *mee* –
thin noodles with fishballs; *wanton mee* – noodles with meat dumplings;
char siu mee – noodles with roast pork; *kon lor mee* – noodles with pork,
liver and prawns; *ho fun* – ribbons of white rice noodles with slices of
shrimp, pork and bean sprouts; *lu mien*, thick noodles with a rich sauce
made of dried prawns, scallops and dried plaice eaten with a touch of
vinegar to remove some of the rich taste; *kway teow* – egg noodles served
with various garnishings. For those who like it hot, there's the *mee rebus*
of the Malays and the slightly spicy *mee siam* of the Nonyas, and *laksa* –
tangy rice noodles cooked in coconut milk with prawn, bean sprouts and
sliced fishballs.

Then there are the clay pot dishes (*sar po*) favored by the Chinese, stuffed bean curd (*niang dou foo*), pork rib soup (*bak kut teh*), fried carrot cakes (*chye tow kway*), spring rolls (*poh piah*), chicken cooked Hainanese style with rice; *satays; soto*, the Malay's hot spicy soup with shredded chicken, bean sprouts and rice cake; oyster omelettes; *lontong* – rice cakes in a rich vegetable curry; *nasi padang* – a type of buffet presentation consisting of small servings of mutton, beef, eggs, vegetables, prawns and fried fish with vegetable curry and rice.

Here are some of the popular hawker centers in Singapore:

Rasa Singapura on Tanglin Road, behind the Singapore Handicraft Centre and close to the Singapore Tourist Promotion Board (for those around the area of the Sheraton Hotel, Ming Court, Orchard Hotel). Among the best of Singapore's hawker stalls, selected for their specialties, are housed here.

Cuppage Centre on Cuppage Road, to which many of the hawkers in the former Orchard Road Car Park have been relocated. The food stalls occupy two floors (the ground floor is a market). The street runs off Orchard road and is located behind Cold Storage. (If you have been looking at the architecture of the old shophouses and bungalows on that street and Emerald Street, this is the place to go. But it does not look as attractive as Rasa Singapura. See also p.102.)

Newton Circle open-air hawker center is also one of the well patronized places serving a wide variety of food. Some food stalls from the Car Park have been re-sited here. Not to be missed are the fruit juice stalls which offer excellent thirst-quenchers.

Telok Ayer Food Centre on Upper Cross Street caters to the office workers in the financial and business district. It is a distinctive Victorian structure, octagonal-shaped with a frame of cast iron. The land on which it stands was reclaimed from the sea in the 1880s. It is near the site where the original brick-built, octagonal-roofed Telok Ayer market stood, built during the days of Sir Stamford Raffles, to provide the people of that day with their supply of fruit, fish, vegetables, poultry and pork. The building was declared a national monument in June 1973.

Queen Elizabeth Walk. In the early days of Singapore this was the Esplanade but reclamation work pushed the sea farther back. This is where you will find the Satay Club which draws patrons fond of satay. It also attracts people who love to eat Malay and Indian Moslem dishes. Over charcoal braziers succulent satays sizzle and the aroma of mutton soup and other delicacies fills the air. The hawkers here also cook *mee rebus, lontong, nasi padang, soto ayam,* curries and *rojak.* For those with a sweet tooth, there are selections of Malay and Chinese desserts.

Boat Quay, another open-air place by the Singapore River. Much of Singapore's early trading took place in this area where boats unloaded their merchandise.

Empress Place, a semi open-air hawker site in a British colonial setting. The buildings around it are the legacies of the British era. It is known for its Indian *rojak*.

Glutton's Corner, located on Tanjong Pagar Road, is for those who would like to sample Indian food.

People's Park, close to Chinatown, has hundreds of stalls offering a wide choice of Chinese dishes.

Haig Road Hawker Centre, near Geylang Serai, specializes in Malay and Indonesian food. A Moslem food stall sells *kacang phool*, an Arabic bread with nuts, onions, chilli, and pepper and which is eaten with eggs or mutton.

Geylang Serai Hawker Centre also serves Malay, Indonesian and *kacang phool*.

Old Airport Road Hawker Centre has a stall open from 9 pm to 1 am which serves bull's penis soup, said to promote circulation of blood. A bull's penis and testicles are steamed for hours with herbs, ginger, salt, pepper and Chinese wine.

Prices. Food in hawker centers is generally cheaper than that obtained in restaurants. Usually signs in the individual stalls indicate the prices of food items. When eating in a hawker center, make the rounds of the stalls to see which food you would like to order. Place your orders directly with the stall owner. Indicate whether you want a large or small serving; whether you want it spicy or not. If you don't want chilli, say so.

Find a table near the stall where you ordered your food. It is best to pay as you order to avoid confusion afterwards. You will be charged according to the number of dishes you order. Servings cost between S$1.50 to $4. Satay is charged by the stick, approximately 30 to 50 cents Singapore each. Check if you are to be charged for satay left uneaten. Pickles, peanuts, Chinese tea or towels are sometimes given to you without your asking for them, then added to your bill afterwards. If you do not like these, refuse at the beginning. If you are not charged for these extras then you should give a tip. Otherwise there is no tipping in hawker centers.

Most hawker stalls will provide you with chopsticks but if you feel more comfortable with fork and knife or spoon, ask for these utensils. True Malay, Indonesian and Indian food is eaten with the hands, especially in places where rice and curries are ladled onto banana leaves. Hands are washed before eating. To eat with the hands: scoop up a small amount of food with your fingers and push the food into your mouth with your thumb. You have to get the hang of it before you feel at ease.

Fresh fruit juice is especially good in hawker centers. A glass of freshly squeezed orange, pineapple, pear, apple, honeydew melon or watermelon juice is good value for money.

Those with a sweet tooth should definitely try these desserts: *Chendol* – a refreshing drink consisting of pale green pandanus jelly

(above) Food stalls in the housing estate at Ang Mo Kiu.
(opposite page) Fresh vegetables sold in street markets.

flavored with palm syrup and coconut milk and topped with crushed
ice; *Bubor cha cha* – yam, gelatin, red beans and jelly in coconut milk and
sweetened with palm sugar; *Ice-kacang* – a mound of shaved ice with red
beans, jelly and syrup, and *Goreng pisang* – whole bananas dipped in
flour and fried. Beancurd with syrup is also delicious, but for most, this
is an acquired taste.

Roadside Stalls and Eateries

Good food is sometimes found in nondescript eateries along
crowded streets and alleys – in Chinatown, Serangoon Road (Little
India), North Bridge Road, Bugis Street . . . .

In **Chinatown**, specifically Trengganu, Mosque, Smith and Banda
Streets, food stalls serve some of the most authentic – and exotic –
Chinese fare to be found in town: rice porridge (*congee* or *djook*) plain or
cooked with chicken, pork, duck or fish; vegetarian dishes, noodles, rice
steamed in a clay pot with pieces of pork or prawns and sesame oil; dim
sum (nibblebits and snacks, consisting of a variety of dumplings and
buns filled with minced pork, beef, shrimps, fish and side dishes). A
restaurant on Mosque Street has been patronized for years by people
who go there for dim sum. For those who crave the unusual, a food stall
on Trengganu Street serves soup (claimed to have aphrodisiac qualities)
of iguana, snake, turtle, crocodile and rabbit. And if you are fond of tea,

梁長春貿易公司
NEOH TIONG CHOON TRADING CO.
竹意乾店

Chinatown is one of the places where you can find herbal tea vendors, a disappearing breed. Various types of brewed teas, some of which are drunk for their medicinal qualities, are poured into glasses, all ready for the customer. The glasses are covered to keep the tea warm.

Little India, which is really a stretch of Serangoon Road, is where you can get authentic North and South Indian food, including a vegetarian meal. Here you will see men making *prata* from a fistful of dough which is stretched until it becomes a thin film about one meter wide. These are fried in griddles and served wither plain or with filling (*murtabak*). Both are excellent for sopping up curry sauces. You can order *dosai*, shish kebab, the spicy mutton soup (*kambing* soup), saffron rice (*nasi biryani*), *mee goreng* and different curries. An assortment of sweets, generally prepared with a cream or milk base, tempts those who like desserts. Some are nutty and crunchy, others soft and chewy.

Food Alley is actually Murray Street which the Urban Renewal Authority has redeveloped. The old houses have been converted into restaurants serving a wide variety of Chinese, Indian and Malay dishes, seafood as well as fast foods. For example, Nº 18 is occupied by **Moti Mahal**, specializing in Kashmiri, Punjabi and Northern Indian meals; Nº 20 is **Beng Hiang**, specializing in Hokkien food; Nº 22 is **Moi Kong Hakka Restaurant**, noted for its fine Hakka food, Nº 24-26 is **Kartini**, serving good Indonesian fare.

Bugis Street is known for its roadside food stalls serving mainly Chinese food. Snake soup is available. Fresh fruits are plentiful and inexpensive.

Albert Street, referred to as "Greedy Street", is for those in search of good Cantonese fare, eaten on tables set up by the roadside. Roast duck, chilli crab, sweet and sour pork, fried curry puffs, and fish porridge are some of the favorites of diners.

Seafood

Time was when the only way to eat good seafood was to traipse to some out-of-the-way open-air restaurant along the coast to have chilli crabs and spicy prawns. In these *makan* places strung along the beach, one ate with one's fingers. Reclamation projects have close down some of the once-popular seafood restaurants, but others still exist – at Upper Beach Road, Bedok, Pasir Panjang and Ponggol – serving chilli crabs, steamed prawns, fried squids, mussels, oysters and crayfish, steamed pomfret and garoupa. There are other places like Jurong which serve seafood. Among these is the **Jurong Sea Food Restaurant** (35 Jurong Pier Road) which serves squid balls fried with bread crumbs, baked crabs, and prawns fried in salt.

Nowadays, visitors need not travel too far from the city center to get good seafood (although some diners with a sense of adventure will still insist on seeking out some obscure restaurant out in the boondocks recommended by friends of friends, and the food may compensate for all their trouble of getting there). Right in town diners in search of new things can try the **Sea Food Theatre**, a new restaurant of the Plaza Hotel (formerly the Merlin) on Beach Road. Diners are served their seafood in a stagey setting, totally different from the rustic seafood places out of town. You can have your fish, shellfish, crabs, prawns and lobsters cooked any way you like: fried, steamed, baked, or grilled. Among the dishes are deep-fried garoupa in spicy sauce and baked mussels in an earthern pot.

Besides the open-air seafood *makan* places, the following restaurants are well known for their superb fresh seafood: **The Islander** (Hyatt Regency Hotel) which serves good chilli crab, steamed fish, curried prawns, baked lobster and chilli squid; **Floral Mile** (Dunearn Rd, along Bukit Timah where potted plants are sold), famous for its charcoal grilled lobster, crabs, crayfish and giant prawns. The crispy fried *sotong* (baby squid) is a must. **Seaview** (779-A Upper East Coast Road) serves good chilli crab in thick soupy sauce of coconut and egg spiced with chilli. Ask for a plate of *roti* (bread chunks) to dip in the sauce. Other specialties: chilli fried mussels, steamed cockles with delicious sauce, steamed or fried prawns. Then there is **Prawn House** (15-17 Tiverton Lane, off Killiney Road).

Western Restaurants

Singapore's first class hotels offer continental food in settings that range from sumptuous to cozy. Among the French restaurants that have attracted the notice of Singaporeans are the Dynasty Hotel's **Vendome**, which serves a combination of classical French dishes with nouvelle cuisine; the Marco Polo's **San Marco** with its unusual game dishes; the Hyatt Regency's **Hugo's**, which has been transformed from a Germanic hunting lodge to a chic French dining room with menus for each of the four seasons, the Hilton's **Harbour Grill**, noted for its gourmet delights, and **Le Rosier** (5th floor, The Octagon, 105 Cecil Street).

Other restaurants that serve European fare are **Chez Bidou** (Ming Court Hotel), **Brasserie La Rotonde** (Marco Polo Hotel); **Belvedere** (Mandarin Hotel), **Le Chalet** (Ladyhill Road), **Chesa** (Hotel Equatorial), **La Ronde** (Hotel Malaysia Singapore), **Baron's Table** (Holiday Inn), **Troika** (DBS Building, 6 Shenton Way), which serves Russian and continental fare, and **Restaurant 1819** (Tuan Sing Restaurant, 30 Robinson Road).

Italian restaurants include **Mario's** (York Hotel, 21 Mount Elizabeth), **La Taverna** (16 Emerald Hill Road, or B17, DBS Bldg, Shenton Way), **Jack's Place** (Yen San Bldg, Orchard Road), **Pete's Place** (Hyatt Regency). All serve pizzas and pastas with Italian wine. Mexican food can be ordered at **De Viennese Restaurant** (Specialists Centre, Orchard Road), **Chico's n Charlie's** (4th Floor, Liat Towers, Orchard Road), and **Ginivy Coffee House** (International Building, Orchard Road), which also serves pizzas along with Mexican food.

The **Beefeater** (417 River Valley Road), is an English-type pub and
restaurant which offers bangers and mash, fish and chips and
English-type pies. **The Stables** (Mandarin Hotel) dishes up English food,
and a good steak tartar.

Steak-eaters can go to: **Cairnhill Steak House** (12-14 Cairnhill
Road), **Emerald Steak House** (115-117 Emerald Hill Road), **Fosters
Steak House** (Amber Mansions), or **Frisco Grill** (601 Orchard Towers,
Orchard Road). Unless you want to be saddled with a huge drinks bill,
take care that you are not unduly detained at the cocktail lounge for
pre-meal drinks.

Places of Interest

The first-time visitor to Singapore out to explore the town can either
sign up for a package tour or see the sights on his own. The standard
City Tour takes about 3-4 hours and covers such points of interest as the
orchid pavilion of the Botanic gardens, Mt. Faber, Tiger Balm Gardens
and gem and batik factories. The tour drives past Queen Elizabeth Walk,
Supreme Court, City Hall, Singapore river, Chinatown and the Sri
Mariamman Hindu Temple. Some tours also stop at the National
Museum or the Singapore Handicraft Centre. Coach tours include the
45-minute *Instant Asia* or the *Singapore Experience* show in the ticket price.
Starting time: 9 am. By coach and by car (maximum four passengers).

The **East Coast Tour** (3-4 hrs) skirts the East Coast. Along the way
one sees the harbor, Marine Parade satellite town and Changi Prison area.
Stops are made at the East Coast recreational park, crocodile farm, the
Temple of 1000 Lights on Race Course Road and Changi Village. Tours
start at 9 am and 2 pm. By coach and by car (maximum four passengers).

Other tours available are the combination of City/East Coast Tour,
Trishaw Tour, Sentosa Island Tour, City and Junk Cruise, City and
Sentosa Tour, harbor and junk cruises. Enquire from the tour desk at
your hotel for prices and for other specialized tours. Those who would
like to explore at their own pace and their own time can do so. These are
among the places of interest in Singapore:

Parks and Gardens

Chinese and Japanese Gardens

The industrial heart of Singapore beats in Jurong. In this satellite
town factories and workshops manufacture the goods for Singapore's
home use and export.

To provide a cool arbor and a retreat for the industrial workers, and
to open up areas for the leisure and relaxation of Singaporeans, the
Jurong Park Project was conceived. Hence, the existence in Jurong of a

An exhibit at the Singapore Zoo's Reptile House.

public park, a Bird Park, and Chinese and Japanese Gardens built around the lake.

The **Chinese garden**, Yu Hwa Yuan, follows a classical design. A pair of marble lions guards the entrance, and an arched white bridge called the White Rainbow Bridge (*Pai Hung Ch'iao)* connects the main gate to a pavilion. The central part of this pavilion is *Yo Lo Yuan* (Fishes Paradise) where goldfish and carp play among the lotus pods. On either side of this fish pool are courtyard gardens of two different styles: one quaint with a bridge and a pond; the other profuse with flowers – jasmine and pomegranates.

Sauntering through the 13.5-hectare (33.3-acres) garden you come across two covered pavilions (described as twin towers) jutting out over the lake near a clump of willows. On the central lake graced with lotus is a stone boat (Moon Inviting Boat) and teahouse. Such delightful features as streams and waterfalls, pools and ponds, graceful bridges, bamboo groves, clumps of tall reeds, stands of pine and ficus trees,and a seven-story pagoda romantically named **Cloud-Piercing Pagoda** are present. Those so inclined can climb the spiral staircase for a bird's eye view of the garden.

Scenic spots have romantic names like *Wan Yueh* (Arbor for Moon-Admiring); *Hsiang Sze Chi Yi* (Place to Convey Lovers' Wishes); *Woh Hu Kang* (Reclining Tiger Mound).

Seiwaen, the Japanese garden, is sited on a 13.5-hectare (33.3-acres) island in Jurong Lake. It was patterned after the Japanese gardens of the late 14th and 15th centuries, when the art of Japanese garden design was at its height, by Prof. Kinsaku Nakane, an authority on this subject. Charming bridges span still ponds and meandering streams, miniature waterfalls trickle down rocks, stone lanterns crown gentle knolls and arrangements of stones add meaning to the landscape. All invite meditation.

Directly in front of you as you enter the garden is the Dry Garden or **Karezansui** with its carefully arranged pattern of pebbles, rocks, pruned shrubs and trees. From there you can take whichever path appeals to you. The path on the right leads to the rest house and the bridge which overlooks the large pond and its beach. The left-hand path goes past the waterfall, summer house and the north side of the large pond. Another path to the left winds past a wisteria trellis, over a stream and across the beach Ginrinsu.

Signs describe the different parts of the garden inviting one to ponder on the special aspects of the scene before one's eyes: *Hiraiho* (The peak where auspicious birds like to gather); *Ryumonbanku* (The waterfall which is the way of a dragon to the sky); *Gaunkyo* (The bridge that lies as if it is in a bed of clouds); *Zesshokei* (The beautiful stream with ceaseless sound); *Kyoyochi* (A very pure and quiet mirror-like pond); *Suiranho* (The freshly verdant, sacred mountain).

The most inspiring time to visit the garden and get the full effect of its serenity is either in the early morning or late afternoon. Midday is not a good time as the heat of the sun tends to spoil one's enjoyment.

A S$2.50 ticket will admit you to both gardens (S$1.20 for a child). A visit to the Japanese garden alone entails an entrance fee of S$1 for an adult and half price for a child. Admission ticket to the Chinese garden is S$2 for adults; S$1 for children. The gardens are open daily from 9 am to 6 pm. Located off Yuan Ching Road in Jurong, they are accessible by bus or taxi. Traveling time by public bus from the Orchard Road area is approximately an hour; by taxi it takes about 30 minutes. Bus Nº 10, 30, 154, 165, 178, 183, 184, 192, 196, 197, 198, 199 will take you to Jurong Interchange. From there take bus Nº 242 (on Sundays and public holidays it's 406) to the gardens.

Jurong Bird Park

Ornithologists and bird-fanciers should take time out to visit the Bird Park on the slope of Jurong Hill. Here, on 20.2 hectares (50 acres) of woodlands, 7000 birds representing more than 350 species roost and nest in ponds, lagoons, paddocks, wetlands and aviaries. Flamingos like skinny-legged ballerinas in short *tutus*, pelicans, swan, geese and other species of waterfowl, and flying birds both big and small are to be seen. The Jurong Bird Park boasts the largest collection of birds from South East Asia and other parts of the world.

The penguins are the first on parade, strutting about like stiff-necked stuffed shirts. There is the Humboldt penguin from South

America, the little blue penguin from South Australia, and the king penguin from the Antarctic region. The penguin house has a regulated temperature to keep the creatures in good health.

The gorgeously plumed macaws, showy parrots and cockatoos, all draped on the tree branches like colorful silk banners can hardly be missed. The low building to the left is the **World of Darkness**. The Jurong Bird Park claims the distinction of being the first aviary in Asia to have a nocturnal bird house.

Birds unseen by man during the day can be observed as they go about their tasks in an atmosphere simulating night. This is achieved by using special lighting effects and recreating the whirr of cicadas and a staccato of bird-calls. As the eyes become accustomed to the gloom, one makes out the horned owls staring wide-eyed in their forest-like settings; the kiwi, New Zealand's flightless national bird, as it prances about in the darkness seeking food; the night herons, the wekas, the frogmouth, and the fruit bats of Southeast Asia hanging upside down in eerie formations like creatures from a haunted house.

Time your visit so that you are in the park for the 10.30 am Bird Show (daily, except Mondays). A flock of low-flying peafowl opens the show. Necks outstretched, they cover the distance from hill slope to stage with a flapping of wings. The next on show are the sharp-sighted kites. At a sign from their trainer they swoop down from their roosts high up in the trees and, in a dazzling show of precision and skill, snatch from mid-air what they are led to believe is a juicy prey. The saucy cockatoos, brilliantly plumed macaws and toucans next display their "intelligence" by answering the telephone and saying "Hello" and "Goodbye" to the spectators.

The climax of the show is the appearance of an eagle with a wing-spread of seven feet who dives down and pounces with unerring skill on its bait. The spectators are advised not to stand while these birds are circling and swooping and to be quiet. Admission to the amphitheater is free. There is also an afternoon show on Sundays and public holidays at 3.30 pm.

Footpaths meander throughout the park for those who prefer to walk. Those who are in a hurry to tour the park can board the tram which girdles the grounds at 15-minute intervals (S$1.00 for adults; S$0.50 for children). One must be prepared to queue up if there is a thick crowd. The tram stops at the **Walk-in Aviary**, claimed to be the biggest in the world. A wire net envelopes the tall-growing trees and jungle covering 2.1 hectares (52 acres) of land. In this haven live many types of birds. The sylvan setting of trees and running streams is enhanced by a 30.5-m (100-ft) high man-made waterfall. Visitors are advised to move quietly and speak softly so as not to disturb the birds.

A restaurant built over the lake serves hot meals and cold drinks. There are also food kiosks scattered throughout the park. If you have the time and inclination, spend a day here. Otherwise, go early in the

(above) A serene moment at the Japanese Garden, Jurong.
(opposite page) The man-made waterfall at Jurong Bird Park.

morning and stay until midday. The park is open from 9 am to 6.30 pm
on weekdays and from 9 am to 7 pm on weekends and public holidays.
Admission fee is S$3.50 for adults and S$1.50 for children 12 years and
below, but this likely to be revised so check first. Organized group tours
of more than 30 people can be given concessions. There is a surcharge of
50 cents Singapore for bringing in a still camera, and S$2 for a movie
camera. It is forbidden to play radios and tape recorders as the sounds
are apt to disturb the birds.

You may take a taxi to the park or ride on the bus. Nº 250 runs from
Jurong Interchange to the Park. For more information, call 2650022.

Ming Village

A center for the production of porcelain and reproduction of period
pieces mainly from the Ming and some from the Ching dynasties is one
of the newest attractions in Jurong. At the Ming Village visitors can
watch the actual process of porcelain production, from the shaping of
the basic molds to the glazing, hand-painting of the design and firing.
Designs range from the classical and traditional to contemporary.
Celadon ware (pink and green) with cracked glaze, Ming imperial ware
in cobalt blue and white, as well as other types of porcelain of the Ming
and China eras are reproduced here. Singaporean artists are encouraged
to use the center as an outlet for their creativity.

Apart from the art studio, the Ming Village has showrooms where finished products are displayed and sold. The standard size Ming and Ching vases fetch an average of S$1000 and reproductions of good period pieces as much as S$50,000. There are a few originals around, one-of-a-kind antique pieces for the art collector if he wishes to buy. At this stage, visitors could well be treated to demonstrations of skills other than pottery in the special handicrafts section. The Ming Village is easily reached via the West Coast Expressway.

Singapore Zoological Gardens

Breakfast al fresco with an orange utan is something to write home about. With pictures to prove it too. This unique experience awaits animal lovers who visit the Singapore Zoological Gardens. The breakfast tour is bookable through a tour operator (enquire from the tour desk in your hotel). You arrive at the zoo in time to have a buffet breakfast at 9 am.

After the *homo sapiens* have had their breakfast, an orang utan is led to one table where a cup of coffee, a glass of fruit juice, a bowl of congee or rice porridge, fruit and rolls await. While the big simian is gulping down glassfuls of fruit juice, munching rolls and eating congee, tour members are invited to sit beside her and be photographed. **Ah Meng,** a 24-year-old adult, and her offsprings are the most photographed orang utan at the zoo. According to the zoo's director, Bernard Harrison, Singapore Zoo has the largest social grouping of orang utan.

After breakfast, you are free to roam as you please. The energetic can walk but most tour members are shepherded into trams which snake through the grounds. Stopping points are the **polar bear enclosure** to see the bears stand up to their full height and hit a ball suspended above them; the **cheetah and lion enclosure**, the enclosure where **sea lions** performs tricks, the **leopard enclosure** and the **orang utan enclosure**. Non-tour members who don't wish to walk can also avail themselves of the tram service (S$1 for adults, 50 cents for children). If time is limited, this is a definite boon. Compared to other zoos, the Singapore Zoo is fairly young. It opened in 1973 but already it has been praised by other zoo directors around the world for its planning and landscaping. More than 1500 animals representing about 150 different species are housed in open enclosures designed to look like their natural habitats. Water, trees and rocks surround the animals, providing a psychological as well as a natural barrier between them and the viewing public. There is a pleasing sense of balance in the way these elements are used. The animals are rendered more inaccessible by distance and height. Thus they are free to range and roam in their natural areas, unencumbered by bars and undisturbed by the public. The only animals enclosed in cages are the dangerous big cats and carnivorous animals.

The latest feature of the zoo is the **Reptile Garden**. Lizards, snakes, turtles, and crocodiles are housed in simulated habitats. The collection includes 50 species of reptiles such as venomous king cobras, adders, vipers, kraits and snakes indigenous to Singapore, and poisonous arrow frogs. Endangered species include the rhinoceros iguana, native to Haiti, which feeds on vegetables and fruit. The adult male grows to a length of 1.5 m (4 feet) and displays a horn on its snout similar to that of a rhinoceros, hence its name.

Another endangered species on display is the Galapagos giant tortoise whose natural habitat is the warm but completely dry lava soils in the lowlands of the Galapagos Islands. These heavyweight creatures (they can weigh as much as 150 kgs or 330 lbs) can grow to about 1.1 m (3.6 ft) in length and are known to live to the ripe old age of 200. the two pairs of Galapagos giant tortoises are a gift from the Honolulu Zoological Gardens.

The zoo added a **penguin exhibit** and **pygmy hippo exhibit** in 1982 and a **gorilla exhibit** in 1983. It also acquired a pair of maned wolves. an endangered species native to South America, the maned wolf is more of a wild dog than a wolf. It is the first of the dog family to be displayed at the Singapore Zoo which is also the first zoo in Asia to displayed maned wolves.

The animal enclosures occupy only 28 hectares (69 acres) of the sprawling 90 hectares (222 acres) of woodland wrapped around the **Seletar Reservoir**. the remainder is used to exhibit botanical specimens. Several rubber trees, grown from seedlings imported from the Peradeniya Botanical Garden in Sri Lanka, have been cultivated to show how rubber is tapped. In the mornings women are to be seen making fresh cuts in the barks of the trees to allow the thin latex liquid to drip into containers.

There is something for everybody who goes to the zoo. Schoolchildren have special outings and for those with young children, it is a good place to spend the day. There are pony rides from 10 am to 12 noon and 2.30 to 4.30 pm on Sundays and public holidays and elephant rides daily from 4 to 4.30 pm and animal shows at 3.30 pm daily, with an extra show at 11 am on Sundays and public holidays. The **Children's Zoo** enables children to touch and hold small and young tame animals. Prices for pony and elephant rides and show-times may change so check with the zoo's public relations officer at tel: 2693411-5.

A canteen within the zoo grounds serves lunch while food kiosks scattered throughout the park offer refreshments.

Located in Mandai, the zoo is about 35 to 40 minutes' drive from the Orchard Road area.If you are not joining a tour group, you can either take a taxi or bus. N° 171 from Queen street via Bukit Timah Road and Woodlands Road, then N° 137 from Toa Payoh via Thomson Road. The drive northward passes rubber plantations and orchid nurseries and skirts the scenic Seletar Reservoir. The zoo is open daily from 8.30 am to 6 pm. Admission fees are S$3.50 for adults and S$1.50 for children.

The arched entrance to the Chinese Garden, Jurong.

Orchid Garden

The tropical climate of Singapore nurtures orchids, and whole nurseries of them occupy hillsides, festooning the surrounding verdure in gorgeous blooms and perfuming the air with their mingled scents. The best and the biggest nursery is in **Mandai**. For the orchid-grower and fancier, this should not be missed.

Four hectares (10 acres) are planted with different varieties of orchids, from the exotic Vandas and spectacular Phalaenopsis to delicate Dendrobiums and Arandas. There are also hundreds of hybrids. Singapore continues to devote time and money to research projects on orchid culture. It is one of the leading orchid centers in the world as well as a major exporter of cut orchids which pull in more than S$18 million in foreign exchange a year.

The garden is open from 9 am to 6 pm daily. Admission is S$1 for adults, S$0.50 for children, refundable if you purchase plants. A taxi or bus will take you there. Traveling time by taxi is approximately 35 minutes from the Orchard Road area, or an hour by public bus. Since the Orchid Garden is near the zoo, you could combine a trip to these places on the same day.

To get there: Take a bus to Bukit Timah, then transfer to another bus for the zoo; or board any of the buses going to Toa Payoh, then change to another bus for the zoo.

Bus Nº 5, 74, 153, 154, 157, 170, 172, 173, 174, 175, 180, 181, 182, 193 and 200 to go to Bukit Timah, passing floral nurseries along the way. Some of these buses will also bring you to the Bukit Timah Nature Reserve.

Bus No. 73, 95, 139, 140, 141, 143, 145, 146, 148, 149, 150, 151, 152, 153, 155, 157, 158, 159 will take you to Toa Payoh, through the industrial town of Jurong. From there, take a 137 bus to the zoo.

Bukit Timah Nature Reserve

A part of the original jungle has been preserved to give those who live in asphalt jungles an idea of what Singapore was like in the early days when tigers roamed about and princes were apt to mistake them for lions. This is Singapore's highest point (177 m/581 ft) and if you are intent on climbing to the summit, be sure you have a pair of strong legs as the going can be rather rough and steep in places. The air is thin there and is not conducive to the unfit. As there are no vehicles to fall back on, hikers can only depend on their own leg power. Footpaths lead to thick growths where you might chance upon a squirrel or civet cat. All around is heard the intense humming of insects. Admission to the nature reserve is free. Along the way you pass what is known as the "Floral Mile" because the highway is bordered by flower nurseries and large trees. Bus Nº 5, 170-173, 177, 180-182, 200.

Macritchie Reservoir

This is a park in a jungle setting which is bordered by a reservoir. Walking along the paved paths and dirt tracks, nature-lovers can catch a glimpse of birds and butterflies. Located on Lornie Road. Can be reached by bus Nº 74, 93, 104, 130, 132, 150, 157, 160-167.

Botanic Gardens

If you want to combine an early morning exercise with some sightseeing, then head for the Botanic Gardens on Cluny and Holland Roads. It's just 10 minutes by taxi or 20 minutes by bus from the hotels in the Orchard Road area. The gardens are a favorite haunt of joggers and *tai chi* exponents – those persons whom you see doing slow motion exercises somewhat like shadow boxing. Admission is free to the public and the gates open as early as 5 am.

While you jog, or walk, look at some of the attractions of the gardens – topiaries in manicured lawns, rockeries and marsh garden, carp-filled lake.

Serious horticulturists, of course, would pay more attention to the trees, ferns, tubers and ornamental plants grown there. Rubber plantations in Southeast Asia owe their existence to the Singapore Botanic Gardens which nurtured the first rubber trees imported as seedlings from Kew Gardens in England. The herbarium is also noteworthy, containing about half a million specimens. One of the tourist attractions is the cannonball tree, so called because its heavy fruits hang like cannonballs from the branches.

One of the most popular sections of the garden is the **orchidarium,** visited by many tourists. In fact city tours start with the Botanic Gardens, bringing tour members to see only the orchid section. This is not large, compared to the orchid gardens at Mandai but it exhibits representative varieties of arandas, arachnis, dendrobiums, oncidiums, phalaenopsis and vandas. On display also is the *Vanda Miss Joachim,* a cross between *Vanda teres* and *Vanda hookeriana.* This hybrid was produced by Miss Joaquim in her garden in 1893 and has since become Singapore's national flower.

Photography buffs will find the Botanic Gardens a source of delight. Gates close at 11 pm but on weekends and public holidays the grounds stay open for visitors up to midnight. The gardens are accessible by Bus Nº 7, 14, 75, 95, 106, 112, 174 and 188.

In the heart of the city are green retreats such as **Central Park** on Clemenceau Avenue. Within its 16 hectares (40 acres) are to be found a floral clock, historic cemetery, the **National Theatre** and the **Van Kleef Aquarium** (open from 9.30 am to 9 pm daily). The aquarium faces River Valley Road. Admission is 60 cents Singapore for adults and 40 cents for children. **Elizabeth Walk** on Connaught Drive is a tree-lined promenade by the sea where the open-air Satay Club, famous for its satays, is sited (see FOOD AND DRINK, p.80). From here one can look across the road to the **Padang,** a large green field where soccer, hockey, softball, and cricket matches are held in the evenings. Across the Padang are the **City Hall** and the **Supreme Court,** built during Singapore's colonial era. At one end of Elizabeth Walk, right at the mouth of the Singapore River, is **Merlion Park** on which stands the eight-meter (26-ft) high statue of the Merlion with the head of a lion and the body of a fish. One can look out over the harbor from this vantage point.

The city parks and the gardens are ideal places to bring children. In addition to these, one can consider visiting the **Tiger Balm Gardens-** (Pasir Panjang Road) which is something like fantasyland with its painted grottoes and mythological animals and figures (open from 8 am to 6 pm; admission free). The **Science Center** (on Science Center Road in Jurong, open 10 am to 6 pm Tuesdays to Sundays; S$1 for adults, 50 cents for children) has presentations fascinating for both young people and adults. The three galleries (life sciences, physical sciences and aviation) are equipped with audio-visual aids to stimulate interest: video and slide shows, multimedia shows, and displays in glass cases. A new feature is the Ecology Garden for outdoor biological and ecological classes.

National Monuments

Old buildings in Singapore are being demolished one by one to give way to urban redevelopment. But some edifices of historic significance have been preserved. These date back to the time of Sir Thomas

Stamford Raffles or were constructed before the turn of the century. Among the national monuments are:

Thian Hok Keng or Temple of Heavenly Bliss on Telok Ayer Street in Chinatown. This is one of the oldest temples in Singapore and is dedicated to Ma Chor-po, queen of heaven and goddess of seafarers. Sailors and newly-arrived immigrants from China in the early 1820s used to light joss sticks there to thank the goddess for a safe journey. The incense house was constructed just on the edge of the sea but reclamation work in the 1880s pushed the shoreline farther away. The present temple was built in 1839-42 with materials brought from China and paid for by donations from grateful devotees.

Nagore Durgha, originally known as Shahul Hamid Durgha, was built by the Moslems of Southern India in 1828-30. Blending the features of Eastern and Western architecture, it exudes an air of ancient decay, as if it has been abandoned to the ghosts of the past. It is located on the same side of the street as the Thian Hok Keng temple.

The **Sri Mariamman Temple** on South Bridge Road is the Hindus' oldest place of worship in Singapore. It is dedicated to the goddess Mariamman, who is also known as Kali, destroyer of demons. Mariamman is one of the nine forms taken by Devi, wife of Siva (the third god of the Indian Trinity). She is invoked for powers to cure illnesses resulting from epidemics, such as cholera, smallpox, chicken-pox etc.

Built in 1827, the original temple was made of wood and attap but was replaced by one of stronger materials. The building and main tower were re-faced and re-decorated in 1832-5, and again in 1971 and in 1980. However, the general layout and core have remained unchanged since 1843. The land on which the temple stands was donated by Naraina Pillay. He was a government clerk who arrived in Singapore with Sir Stamford Raffles in 1819 aboard the *Indiana*, and subsequently became a building contractor, textile merchant and a Captain of the Tamil Hindus.

On a Tuesday Hindu maidens go to the temple to pray for good husbands while mothers visit to ask for favors or give thanksgiving for favors granted. On special occasions, the entrance to the temple is decorated with banana plants, mango leaves and coconuts. Priests dressed in dhotis offer the prayers of the supplicants and light a fire to the deity. Then the supplicants are blessed with sacred ashes and given bananas and coconuts and jasmine blossoms. Take off your shoes before entering this temple.

Masjid Al-Abrar on Telok Ayer Street was built in 1827 for the Chulias, the Moslems from southern India. It is nicknamed *kuchu* (hut) *pali* (mosque) because of its original humble construction. The present building of brick dates back to 1850-55. The mosque is under the trusteeship of the Mohammedan and Hindu Endowment Board.

The **Sultan Mosque** on North Bridge Road is Singapore's biggest mosque. Its glinting onion dome dominates the immediate

The Supreme Court with its Corinthian columns.

neighborhood two-story buildings. It was constructed in 1924-48 on the site of another mosque built a century earlier, before North Bridge Road was extended beyond Arab Street. The East India Co. donated $3000 towards the construction of the original mosque. Part of the land was leased to the mosque's trustees by Tengku "Alam Sultan" Ala'u'd-din'Alam Shah (proclaimed by a few hundred Malays and Bugis of Kampong Glam as King of Johor and Pahang on 11 january 1879). Another part was conveyed by Tunku Aleema on 20 April 1879.

Carpeted and chandeliered, the mosque displays other modern touches; the most noticeable is a digital clock indicating the time in Singapore and Mecca. There is a large upper gallery for women devotees. As in the case of Hindu temples, visitors remove shoes when entering a mosque.

The Anglican **Cathedral of St Andrew's,** with its slender spire soaring skywards, is located on Coleman St, named for the architect and first superintendent of public works, George Drumgoole Coleman. He built the original church on the same site in 1835-6. This was replaced in 1842 by one which was designed by J.T. Thomson, a government surveyor. The tower and spire was struck twice by lightning between 1845 and 1849. The building was considered unsafe and torn down in 1855. The foundation stone for the third and present church building was laid on 4 March 1856 by the Rev. Daniel Wilson, Lord Bishop of Calcutta. Convict labor was used for the construction and the church was consecrated on 25 June 1862.

A detail from a Hindu temple.

The Catholic **Cathedral of Good Shepherd** on A. Queen Street was
built between 1843-6 by Denis Lesley McSwinney, a merchant and
contractor who went to Singapore in 1828. At about the time the tower and
spire of St. Andrew's were struck by lightning, a tower and spire were
added to the Good Shepherd in 1847 by Charles Alexander Dyce, high
sheriff for Malacca, Penang and Singapore and who arrived as a merchant
from India in 1842. The nave was extended by three bays in 1887 and the
cathedral was consecrated in 1897 by the Bishop of Malacca, Rev. Rene Fee.
The name Good Shepherd was inspired by the French missionary Laurence
Imbert, Bishop of Korea who, arrested in the 1830s during the
anti-Christian campaign, exhorted his parishioners to escape, saying that
the Good Shepherd was ready to lay down his life for his flock.

The Armenian **Church of St Gregory the Illuminator** on Armenian
Street was designed and built in 1835 by George Coleman, builder of the
first St Andrew's Church. The circular structure was inspired by
St Martin's-in-the-Fields in London. It is superimposed by a square plan
with projecting square porticoes on four sides. Originally the building
had an octagonal cone roof surmounted by a bell turret with eight arches
supported by eight Ionic columns, but in 1847 the turret was replaced by
a square one with four Doric pilasters. The bell tower was removed in
1853 by the English architect Maddock who also replaced the pitched
roof and added the east portico round the original chancel to support the
present tower and spire. The church is no longer used for services.

Sri Perumal Temple on Serangoon Road is situated on a piece of land which the East India Co sold to Mr Narasinghan in 1855 for 21 rupees and three annas (equivalent to S$380 in present-day terms). A *madapam* or main hall was incorporated in the original structure. There was also a large pond which was closed in the 1920s for environmental reasons. Well-known sculptors from South India were invited to design the motifs on the temple roofs. The 20-metre high *gopuram* (monumental gateway) is oblong in shape and tapers at the top. Carvings of the various manifestations of Lord Vishnu, the temple's main deity, decorate each of the gopuram's five tiers. The structure, begun in 1977, took two years to complete. This temple is dedicated to Vishnu, one of the three gods of the Hindu Trinity and the preserver of the universe. Several important festivals are held here (see FESTIVALS, pp.57-70).

Hong San Kee is an imposing structure standing on a hill along Mohamed Sultan Road. The people from Lam Ah township of Fujian province in South China bought the land and the temple was erected between 1908 and 1913 from materials brought in from China. The temple attracts a large number of worshipers.

Telok Ayer Market on Raffles quay stands on 8035 sq m (9,611 sq miles) of land reclaimed from the sea. It is a typically Victorian building, octagonal in shape with a cast-iron frame. Built in 1894 and restored in 1973, it now houses the famous Telok Ayer Food Centre. The original market stood on a spot close to where Cecil Street joins Market Street. Made of brick with a tiled roof, it was also octagonal in shape with a diameter of 36.6 m (120 ft). It was Raffles who proposed to the Town Committee to have one market which would house under its roof the fish, pork, poultry, vegetable and fish sellers. This was done to make it easier for the police to patrol the area and for the convenience of both the shoppers and the cleaners.

The former **mansion of Tan Yeok Nee** on 207 Clemenceau Avenue, distinguished by its carvings and granite pillars, is the only remaining example of a house built in the architectural style of buildings prevalent in Southern China towards the end of the 19th century. It was originally the residence of a wealthy Teochew merchant named Tan Yeok Nee who enjoyed extensive rights of land tenure to cultivate gambier and pepper in Singapore and Johor. The occupants abandoned the house when the railway line to Kuala Lumpur was being laid along what was then Tank Road. Later it was occupied by the station master. In 1912 the government handed over the house in trust to the Rev. Ferguson Davis, Bishop of Singapore, who converted the house into St Mary's House and School for Girls. The Salvation Army bought it for its headquarters in 1940. Damaged by the Japanese during the war, the Salvation Army repaired it but did not alter the structure, retaining its original facade.

Other temples and places of worship worth noting are:

Temple of 1000 Lights on Race Course Road has a gigantic (15-m/49-ft high) Buddha surrounded by thousands of bulks which are lit during religious ceremonies, such as Vesak Day (see FESTIVALS, p.64). Two tiger carvings guard the entrance. A piece of bark from the ancient Bodhi tree under which the Buddha was believed to have attained enlightenment, and a replica in mother-of-pearl of the Buddha's footprint (the original is seen in Adam's Peak, Sri Lanka) are among the relics in the temple. The story of Gautama's search for enlightenment is depicted in a series of pictures at the base of the pedestal. The temple opens at 9 am and closes after the prayers at 4.30 pm.

The most vivid impression one has on visiting this temple is the presence of so many vendors selling religious trinkets, oranges and apples (presumably for altar offerings) and sundry items including postcards inside the temple itself. To get there: take any bus that goes along Serangoon Road and get off just before Lavender Street, then walk to Race Course Road.

The **Leong San Temple** (or Dragon Mountain Temple) also on Race Course Road is dedicated to Kuan Yin, the goddess of mercy. It has a colorful ornamented facade. This temple, too, abounds with vendors.

The highly ornate **Siong Lim Temple** on Jalan Toa Payoh, set like a jewel in the middle of a vast garden, is considered one of the most beautiful Buddhist temples in Singapore. The inner hall enshrines the image of Buddha and behind the main hall is the shrine of the Goddess of Mercy, Kuan Yin. Two Hokkien merchants from Amoy in China donated the money to build the temple in 1902. It is visited by thousands of Buddhist worshipers.

Old Neighborhoods

In Raffles' time, Singapore was divided into zones, demarcating the places where the Chinese, Indians and Malays lived and conducted their business. These old neighborhoods still exist, remnants of the colonial era. Chinatown started in the Telok Ayer Basin in the 1820s, moving westwards to the other side of the Singapore River, but each wave of immigrants from China kept their regional distinctions and maintained their own customs and lifestyles. Indian traders in search of gold spices stopped in Singapore to wait out the monsoon season and then stayed on. When the government set up a brick kiln and lime pit in the area, more workers, their ranks swollen by convict labor, arrived and settled in great numbers, giving the area its name: Little India. Arab Street was the haven of Arab traders who, in the 18th century, were already bringing in rice, coffee, sugar, spices, tobacco, brassware, and batik aboard their square-rigged sailing vessels.

A saunter through these old neighborhoods will give an idea of the atmosphere of Singapore in the 19th century. Two-story shophouses and dwellings lean against each other in cramped streets spilling with merchandise and cluttered with people. Some are in a sad state of disrepair.

(above) Old neighbourhoods showing houses with brick rooftops
(opposite page) The Buddha at the Temple of 1000 Lights, Race Course Road.

The government is not unaware of the historic value of these old neighborhoods and has embarked on their preservation. The houses on **Cuppage Road**, for example, have been restored and preserved as historic relics. The street where Cuppage Centre is located was once a dirt road leading to the residence of William Cuppage, a young European civil servant whose house sat on a hill. In the 1900s, wealthy Chinese merchants set up shop along the street and built houses. The architectural style of the buildings was a mixture of Chinese and European, unique to the Straits Settlements. Chinese-style roofs and verandahs formed a covered passage on each side of the street. Pedestrians can stroll the short length of the street to see the terraced houses which still retain their wooden beams and walls and ceiling fans. Although the interiors can be modernized, permission has to be sought from the government if the occupants of the buildings want to make any changes of the facade. Near Cuppage Road is Emerald Road, where many of the old Malaccan-style houses still stand today.

Chinatown is a maze of streets starting from Telok Ayer and embracing such streets as Mosque, Trengganu, Smith, Banda and Sago Lane. Within this area are open markets selling fruits, vegetables, meat, fish, poultry, provisions, as well as live reptiles, turtles, snakes, mice, bats in baskets and cages, all meant for the dining table. There are cooked food stalls, temples and mosques (described in this chapter); fortune-tellers,

calligraphers, letter-writers and carvers, embalmers and funeral parlors, coffin-makers, repair men, and numerous shops selling a variety of merchandise: porcelain, Chinese medicine and herbs, clothing, cassette tapes, and paper replicas of houses, cars, etc. that are used in Chinese festivals like Ching Ming and Hungry Ghosts (see FESTIVALS). Chinatown is particularly interesting to visit during Chinese festivals when street operas are part of the scene. It is just as fascinating a place to visit during non-festival times. The morning and night markets are a study in contrast.

Serangoon Road's nickname "Little India" is well understood, but the origin of Serangoon is more obscure. It is said that the place was a marshy swamp more than a century ago, inhabited only by long-legged birds called *ranggong;* hence its name. Others say insects – or *serangai –* infested the swamps. **Little India** is where most Indians go to buy their provisions and needs: embroidered and sequinned silk saris, laces, and brocades, incense sticks, household wares, garlands and flower petals for temple offerings, weddings and other religious ceremonies, charms and potions, Indian sweets and cakes. There are places selling chapatis and curries, yoghurt drinks and vegetarian food and restaurants serving traditional North and South Indian dishes. The smell of spices mingles with other scents. Housewives come here to have their spices ground and rice milled. Hindu temples are part of the neighborhood. The most outstanding here is the Sri Perumal Temple, described earlier.

Arabs and Malays have been culturally and commercially interlinked since the 13th century. Arab dhows used to bring in merchandise from other parts of the world and these found their way into the shops along **Arab Street**. Today one can still see spice merchants, carpet and rug sellers, jewelry shops stocked with rubies from Burma, topaz from India, zircons and sapphires and cat's eyes. There are batiks from Indonesia, brassware, straw and cane products, porcelain. Close by is the Sultan Mosque and the sellers of Malay delicacies and *kropeks,* those crackling shrimp and fish crisps. The area beyond Arab Street was **Kampong Glam**, a Malay village where the Sultan of Johor and his followers lived.

Thieves Market: Singapore's version of a Flea Market and Portobello Road is Thieves Market along Sungei Road, a noisy, overcrowded bazaar of narrow lanes lined with stalls selling all sorts of merchandise, some, no doubt, stolen. Several times the government ordered the hawkers to move. To bring home the point that they were serious, workers from the Environment Ministry tore down the makeshift sheds and roadside stalls. But time and again, like the proverbial bad penny, the hawkers kept creeping back. Only time will tell whether the government will finally succeed in re-siting them. In the meantime, visitors can still take a look at this colorful part of Singapore which refuses to die. Stroll there in the early evening when business tend to be brisk. It is not suggested that one should buy anything in this market, but it is worth a visit for local color.

Raffles Hotel on Bras Basah and Beach Roads is closely associated
with the colonial history of Singapore. Built in French Renaissance style,
it is one of the landmarks of a bygone age, made famous by such writers
as Somerset Maugham, Rudyard Kipling, Joseph Conrad and Noel
Coward. It was here in the hotel's Long Bar that the Singapore Gin Sling
was concocted.

The hotel was originally a bungalow occupied by a Captain and Mrs
Dare. In those days, Beach Road was a residential area, with elegant
houses fronted by gardens. As the colony grew and more ships were
calling at Singapore, the necessity to provide accommodation became
imperative. At first the Dares found themselves serving lunches. Soon
their bungalow became known as a tiffin house and gradually it turned
into a hostel.

When the Sarkies brothers, hoteliers from Armenia, took over the
hostelry, it became known as the Raffles Hotel. Extensions were added
to the original building in the late 19th century and by the early 1900s,
Raffles Hotel was one of the centers for social events and entertainment,
along with the **Grand Hotel de l'Europe**, now defunct. High-ranking
Japanese officials made it their quarters during World War II, and at the
end of the war it sheltered refugees from Java and the East Indies. The
hotel declined after the war and it was only in the 1970s that the hotel
management made a move to restore it to its original state.

The **National Museum** on Stamford Road combines Victorian and
Palladian features of architecture. It has preserved the classical pillars,
Doric orders and coat-of-arms of Queen Victoria. Established in 1849, it
was originally known as the Raffles Museum until the change of name in
1960. Today it is the repository of Singapore's cultural heritage, housing
more than 21,000 items of archaeological, ethnological and historical
materials.

Notable among the collections are prehistoric implements and
artifacts dating back to the Old Stone Age and extending to the
Indianization of peninsular Malaysia in the 12th century; a fragment of
Singapore stone with Kawi inscriptions, representing that period of the
nation's history when it was part of the powerful Majapahit Empire; coins
of the region in use from the 11th century onwards; Chinese and Southeast
Asian ceramics; Indian and Southeast Asian sculptures. The jade collection
formerly seen in the Jade House is now housed in the museum.

There are various paintings and lithographs of scenes of Old
Singapore, portrait paintings of former governors and one of Sir Thomas
Stamford Raffles based on the original done in 1817 by G.F. Joseph.
Contemporary paintings by Singaporean artists are also on display as
well as children's art in the Young People's Gallery.

The museum's ethnological collection shows the cultures of
Southeast Asian countries. There is also an exhibit of furniture,
household utensils, costumes and garments of Singaporeans of the past.

Historic Landmarks

Like other cities, Singapore has several historic landmarks. At Empress Place stands the 2.43-meter (eight feet) tall **bronze statue** of Sir Thomas Stamford Raffles, called "The Iron Man" by the early Malays. Sculptor Thomas Woolner, R.A. depicts the founder of Singapore with his head bent a little, as if in thought, arms folded, and with a map of the settlement at his feet. The statue was erected at the Esplanade (now the Padang) close to the enclosure before that area was reclaimed from the sea, and unveiled during the Golden Jubilee celebration of Queen Victoria's reign on 27 June 1887. The statue was transferred to its present site during the centenary celebration of Singapore's founding. Very few people are aware of the fact that on the south side of the north aisle of Westminster Abbey in London there is a large statue of Raffles with this inscription:

To the memory of Sir Thomas Stamford Raffles, L.L.D., F.R.S.,
Lieutenant-Governor of Java
And First President of the Zoological Society of London,
Born 1781. Died 1826.
Selected At An Early Age to Conduct the Government
Of the British Conquests in the Indian Ocean
By Wisdom, Vigor and Philanthropy.
He Raised Java to Happiness and Prosperity
Unknown Under Former Rulers.
After the Surrender of That Island to the Dutch
And During His Government in Sumatra
He Founded an Emporium at Singapore
Where in Establishing Freedom of Person
As the Right of the Soil
And Freedom of Trade as the Right of the Port
He secured to the British Flag
The Maritime Superiority of the Eastern Seas.
Ardently Attached to Science
He Laboured Successfully to Add to the Knowledge
And Enriched the Museums of His Native Land.
Promoting the Welfare of the People Committed to His Charge
He Sought the Good of His Country and the Colony of God.

The Victoria Theatre and Memorial Hall, built in the honor of Queen Victoria, has a **clocktower**, described as Singapore's "Big Ben". The clock, with a face measuring 3.6 m (12 ft) in diameter, was installed in 1906. On only three occasions in its history has it stopped marking time: in 1922 and 1936 due to damage caused by rainwater and in 1942 due to bombing before the city fell to the Japanese. (Workmen sprucing up the

The statue of Sir Thomas Stamford Raffles, Empress Place.

building for the Prince of Wales' visit in 1922 allowed rainwater to seep in, thus damaging its internal mechanism. Damage due to rain was again responsible for its stoppage in 1936.) The Victoria Theatre is the present home of the Singapore Symphony Orchestra.

Along tree-lined Connaught Drive is the **Cenotaph**, dedicated to the memory of the Allied Forces who died during World War I and II. The monument was unveiled by the then Prince of Wales (later Duke of Windsor) during his visit to Singapore in 1922. Beside the cenotaph is a **fountain** of Victorian design built in 1882 as a gesture to Mr Tan King Seng. This Chinese philanthropist donated S$13,000 to the government in 1857 to ensure an abundant supply of fresh water to the town but only when the island was struck by a severe drought was the money used. By then, of course, it was too late. Out of shame, it is said, the fountain was built.

Another landmark is the 67-m (220-ft) high **War Memorial** on Beach Road. Set in a 1.2-hectare (three acres) parkland, it was built in honor of the thousands of civilians who lost their lives during the Japanese occupation. The four columns, tapering towards the top, stand for the four distinct cultures that make up Singapore's population. Underneath the column is a chamber which contains the ashes of the civilian war casualties. Special memorial services are held here every 15th of February.

Three government buildings of interest are the Parliament House, Supreme Court and City Hall. **Parliament House** is the oldest government building in Singapore. It stands on the site of the village where the Temenggong and the Malays lived in *attap* huts at the time of Raffles' landing.

The **City Hall** – seat of government – was erected in 1929 on the spot where the house of Thomas Church, the first Resident Councilor of Singapore, stood. The house was designed by architect George Coleman, the same man who drew the blueprint of St Andrew's Church. The City Hall was the setting for the signing of the Japanese surrender document in 1945 and the declaration of Singapore's independence as a sovereign state in 1965.

Of more recent vintage is the **Supreme Court**, constructed in 1939 on the piece of land once graced by the presence of the grand Hotel de l'Europe, the venue of many gala social events in the colony before it was demolished in 1936. The Supreme Court is notable for its Corinthian columns and the carvings of the Italian artist Cavaliere Rodolfe Nolli on the tympanum. The figure of Justice is seen in the central panel; another figure symbolizes deceit and violence, and legislators are seen with books in hand asking for justice. Other carvings portray how prosperity is achieved through law.

In front of the Supreme Court and City Hall is an expanse of green field where men may be seen playing cricket in the afternoons. This stretch of green, known as the **Padang** (the Malay word for open playing field) is very much a part of Singapore's colonial history, a focal point

where Singaporeans congregate on important occasions to watch
National Day parades or listen to political rallies and speeches.

In the days when the Padang was known as the Esplanade and the
Hotel de l'Europe and not the Supreme Court overlooked the playing
field, people watched sporting matches of cricket, lawn balls, tennis,
rugby, hockey, even wrestling and horse-racing held during the annual
New Year Day Sports and Regatta. Spectators used to be regaled by
other amusements as well, such as three-legged races, sack races, etc.
The Esplanade then was quite close to the sea. Later, reclamation work
pushed out the sea and added more area to the Padang.

At one end of the field is a colonial-style building with brick
extensions. This is the **Singapore Cricket Club**, an institution on the
island republic. The clubhouse was built in stages during the last quarter
of the last century and has undergone some changes and interior
refurbishing but it stands as a comforting reminder to those who would
hold fast the disappearing landmarks of a bygone era in the midst of all
the urban development taking place in Singapore today.

Excursions from Singapore

From Singapore the magical islands of **Indonesia**, the sun-drenched
beaches and cool mountain resorts of **Malaysia**, the klongs and wats of
Thailand and the rice terraces and island resorts of the **Philippines**
beckon. These are only a few hours away by plane.

Malaysia is Singapore's nearest neighbor, connected to the
peninsula by a 1.1-km (0.68-mile) long causeway. One can reach
Malaysia by rail, air, road and sea. There are coach tours to **Johor Bahru**
and **Malacca**, and combination coach and boat trip to **Pulau Tioman** and
train trips to **West Malaysia**. There are also package air tours to **Penang,
Kuala Lumpur, Genting** and **Cameron Highlands** and, farther afield,
Sarawak and Sabah. Explore the possibilities of hiring a car. This would
be an ideal way of seeing the variegated countryside with its plantations
of rubber and pineapple, rice fields, stretches of beach and mountain
chains.

Johor Bahru, the southernmost town in Malaysia, is the nearest
place to visit from Singapore. Tour groups tarry here to see the **Sultan's
palace** and the **mosque**, watch a demonstration of rubber tapping in one
of the rubber plantations and see women at work weaving sarongs or
doing cottage crafts in one of the Malay houses.

Historic Malacca, famous in the 14th century as a sea port, is also on
the tour itinerary. You have time to wander around the ancient town
with its overlay of Chinese, Portuguese, Dutch and Malay cultures.

Kuala Lumpur, the capital of Malaysia, is a city of mosques and
colonial-style buildings. You can reach it by train or by plane. The train
goes north to **Butterworth**, then across the Thai border to Bangkok. A
trip across the sea from Butterworth brings you to the charming island of

Covered Vase

Carved in the form of a mountain encircled by
figures of children who hold plants of good omen,
such as the Lotus, Peony and Mythical Fungus
(Lingzhi).

J 0017

(above) Exhibits at the Ethnic Hall, National Museum.
(oppsoite page) Carved jade vase seen at the House of Jade.

Penang with its quaint funicular railway going up to Penang Hill, colonial Georgetown, markets and temples.

Mountain resorts like **Genting Highlands**, 1,711 m (5,614 ft) above sea level, with its gambling casinos and modern hotels; **Fraser's Hill** with its golf course and colonial-style bungalows, and **Cameron Highlands** draw many visitors.

Malaysia's **East Coast** has stretches of beautiful beaches, and fishing villages: **Kelantan** (famous for its kite-flying and its decorated fishing boats), **Trengganu, Kuantan, Cherating** and deserted beaches which are the breeding grounds of giant turtles. Time your visit to avoid the monsoon season. In the western part of peninsular Malaysia, the monsoon is from September to December; in the East Coast is is from October to February.

The fishing village of **Mersing**, three hours' drive from Singapore, is a good jump-off point to the unspoiled, palm-fringed islands of Tioman and Rawa, or Pulau Tioman and Pulau Rawa, as they are called, off Malaysia's East Coast. These are ideal get-away places for lazing in the sun, snorkeling, scuba-diving, and deep-sea fishing.

Pulau Tioman is an island of mountainous jungles, beaches and coral reefs. It has a small population (1700) who still live in traditional *kampongs* or villages. A ferry shuttles from the quay at Mersing to the island, negotiating the distance in about 3 hours. Small planes take visitors to the island in 20 minutes. There is a hotel on the island with air-conditioned rooms and facilities for water sports, as well as tennis, archery and football. But those with a flair for adventure (with an eye on their pocketbook) have been known to obtain bed and board in the village *kampongs*. Other holiday-makers have roughed it up camping on the beach and they attest to having a wonderful time, unmolested by mosquitoes. But if you want to be safe, bring along a mosquito repellent and those with sensitive stomachs need to stock up on tablets.

The other island – **Pulau Rawa** – is also pristine and is waters teem with marine life. Boats can be arranged to take visitors to the offshore reef. Chalets on stilts and Malaysian-style bungalows provide accommodation of a rustic nature. Seafood is good on the island and guests can have Malay, European or Chinese dishes to order. A regular ferry service operates between Mersing and Rawa for about M$12 return.

It is possible to see these places without joining group tours. Hiring a car is one way of seeing Malaysia. Going by taxi is another. Surprisingly, taxis can be hired for traveling to the next town or to a place hundreds of kilometers away. Taxis are usually to be found in the vicinity of train stations and bus terminals. Always negotiate price in advance. Find out if other people are going to the same destination. You can economize by taking the same taxi and sharing the expense. By taxi from Johor Bahru to Mersing, for instance, costs around M$40.

From Singapore one can also take a cruise to **Bali** and **Surabaya**, along sea lanes which the ships of old might have taken when Singapore was just Tumasek, a little fishing village by the sea.

Singapore a Century Ago . . .

Glimpses of what life was like in Singapore in the colonial days are provided by Charles B. Buckley, Joanna and Donald Moore, Song Ong Siang, John Cameron and others. In his book, *Our Tropical Possessions in Malayan India*, was published in London in 1865, John Cameron descries the day to day life among the European community in the colony:

"Most of the bungalows are within two miles from town; nearly all, at least, are within hearing range of the 68-pounder gun on Fort Canning, the discharge of which each morning at five o'clock ushers in the day. This is the accepted signal for all old residents to start from bed. The younger, however, indulge in an extra half-hour's slumber. Still, six o'clock generally sees all dressed and out of doors, in the delicious coolness of the morning, before the sun's rays become disagreeably powerful. The air at this hour is that temperature which may be described as a little colder than cool, and it has a sharpness which I have experienced only in the early mornings of tropical countries, or on a frosty day at home.

"Most people limit their walks to two miles, or about half an hour but this is by no means a rule. Some go as far as four, five, or six miles in a morning; these are the early birds who start at gun-fire sharp, and they are in the minority . . .

"During the training season for the races, it is at this hour that the horses are taken their rounds, and the course then forms to a great many the limit of their walk. As early as half-past four the syces or native grooms are up preparing their horses and start a little after gun-fire for the course, a distance of about two miles. At sunrise the horses commence to go their rounds, and as they wait their turns, it is generally half-past six before all have been exercised. As the distance is to most a tolerably long one, the stewards provide tea on the course, so that it is altogether a very favourite resort for about six weeks before both the spring and autumn meetings . . .

"On coming home from these morning rounds, the custom is to get into loose, free and easy attire, generally baju and pajamas. A cup of coffee – or tea, with biscuit, or bread-and-butter and fruit, is then consumed, and the next two hours spent in reading, writing, or lolling about in the verandahs which front each apartment of a house. I have said reading, writing, or lolling about but, more correctly speaking, the time is devoted to a combination of the first and the last. In the daily avocation of most, the pen is pretty actively handled; and unless at mail times, or by those of a literary turn of mind, it is seldom taken up out of office. Reading is generally accomplished in the extremely reclining posture for which the verandah chairs of Singapore are so admirably adapted.

"At half-past eight the breakfast dressing gong or bell is sounded. A gentleman's toilette in this part of the east is not an elaborate one, and half an hour is ample for its completion. The bath is its chief feature. Attached to the dressing-room of each bedroom in almost all houses is a bath-room, with brick-tiled floor, containing a large bathing jar holding about sixty of seventy gallons of water. The orthodox manner of bathing is to stand on a small wooden grating close to the jar, and with a hand bucket to dash the water over the body. This is by no means such an unsatisfactory method as to the uninitiated it may appear. The successive shocks to the system which are obtained by the discharge of each bucketfull of water seems to have a much more bracing effect than that of one sudden and continued immersion. Every gentleman has his native boy or body servant, whose sole duty it is to attend upon him personally. While waiting, this boy lays out his master's apparel for the day; so that on coming from the bath a gentleman has little trouble to get himself attired. As to shaving, the process is generally performed by itinerant Hindoo barbers who for the small charge of a dollar or a dollar and a half per month come very morning round to the residences of their customers. The charge is so small and the saving in trouble so great, that almost all avail themselves of the convenience.

(overleaf) View of city and Singapore River with OCBC Building at left.

Claret for Breakfast

"The universal breakfast hour is nine o'clock, and when the bell then rings the whole household assemble, and should there be ladies of the number this is the first time of their appearance. Singapore breakfasts, though tolerably substantial and provided with a goodly array of dishes, are rarely dwelt over long, half an hour being about the time devoted to them. A little fish, some curry and rice, and perhaps a couple of eggs, washed down with a tumbler or so of good claret, does not take long to get through and yet forms a very fair foundation on which to begin the labors of the day. After breakfast the conveyances drive round to the porch or portico and having received their owners hasten on to town. No matter how many may reside together, each bachelor has generally his own 'turn-out'. And for half an hour each morning the two bridges leading across the river into town present an endless string of these rather motley vehicles . . .

"Arrived in town, ten minutes or a quarter of an hour are usually spent in going the rounds of the square to learn the news of the morning. These commercial square gatherings are quite a characteristic of the place and of the community, and whatever channels they may open to the flow of local gossip, purpose of an open air and non commercial exchange.

"But there are two evenings in the week when the whole European community may generally be seen upon the esplanade, whether or not they be fives or cricket-players, and these are band evenings, generally Tuesdays and Fridays. The band, which is that of the regiment on the station at the time, or from one of the men-of-war which occasionally visit the port, plays on a raised mound on the centre of the esplanade green. The chains which protect the green on ordinary occasions are on these evenings let down and carriages, horsemen, and pedestrians are alike admitted to the greensward. Gathered round the band in a tolerably broad circle are the beauty and fashion of the place. The ladies, to whom almost all the other outdoor amusements are denied, partake at least in this, and though the ruddy glow of the colder latitudes has fled from most cheeks, still there supervenes a languid softness which is more interesting and perhaps more beautiful. The pretty pale-faced European children too may on these occasions be seen tripping about in playfulness a little less boisterous, but quite as cheerful as it witnessed at home. The band plays from half-past five till half-past six, at which hour it is all but dark, when the carriages make for home in a long string gradually falling off one by one as the various residences are reached.

"Except on band nights however, most of the commercial and all of the official world retire home a little before six o'clock. Arrived there, probably a glass of sherry and bitters will anticipate the refreshing process of dressing for dinner. A slight difference as to dinner-hour prevails; some dine at half-past six, some at seven; the former however, is the time most commonly adopted.

Clockwork Regularity

"There is one advantage here which is too seldom to be found in other parts of the world. Whatever may be the hour, a clock-work regularity and punctuality is observed, and this is not with respect to dinner only, but with respect to all other meals. No doubt this regularity also has its share in the maintenance of the good health of the European community.

"Dinner in Singapore is not the light airy meal which might reasonably be imagined from the nature of the climate; on the contrary, it is quite as substantial a matter of fact as in the very coldest latitude. The difference is not that the substantials are fewer, but that the luxuries are more numerous. Indeed the every-day dinner of Singapore, were it not for the waving punkahs, the white jackets of the gentlemen, and the gauzy dresses of the ladies, the motley array of native servants, each standing behind his master's or his mistress' chair, and the goodly display of Argand lamps, might not unreasonably be mistaken for some more special occasion at home. Soup and fish generally precede both the substantials, which are of a solid nature, consisting of roast beef or mutton, turkey or capon, supplemented by side-dishes of tongue, fowl, cutlets or such like together with an abundant supply of vegetables, including potatoes nearly equal to English ones grown in China or India, and also cabbages from Java. The substantials are invariably followed by curry and rice which forms a characteristic feature of the tables of Singapore, and though Madras and Calcutta have long been famed for the quality of their curries, I nevertheless think that those of the Straits exceed any of them in excellence. There are usually two or more different kinds placed on the table and accompanying them are all manner of sambals or native pickles and spices, which add materially to the piquancy of the dish.

"During the progress of the substantials and of the curry and rice, the usual beverage is beer, accompanied by a glass or two of pale sherry. The good folks of Singapore are by no means inclined to place too narrow restrictions on their libations, and it has been found in the experience of older residents that a liberality in this respect conduces to good health and long life. Besides this the American Tudor Company keeps up a tolerably regular supply of ice, and as it is sold as three cents, or less than one and a half per pound, it is within the reach of all, and is an invariable adjunct to all beverages.

Fruit in Abundance

"To curry and rice succeeds generally some sort of pudding or preserve, but sweets have not the same temptation here as at home. Very good cheese however, is obtained in fortnightly supplies by the overland steamers and, as good fresh butter is always to be had, this part of dinner is well enjoyed, accompanied as it is by no illiberal allowance of excellent

JALAN BUKIT M

AH 0315

pale ale. But it is in the luxuriance of the dessert perhaps more than anything else that the tables of Singapore are to be distinguished, and it is little wonder that it should be so; for there is no season of the year at which an abundance of fruit cannot be obtained. Pineapple may be considered the stock fruit of the island, and one or two splendid specimens of these generally adorn the table. There are plantains, ducoos, mangoes, rambutans, pomeloes, and mangosteens. The latter fruit is peculiar to the Straits of Malacca and to Java, and so great is its fame that to India or China no present or gift from Singapore is more acceptable than a basket of them. It is of a somewhat singular genus; it is round, of the size of a small orange, is covered with a thick woody purple bark in place of rind, which has to be cut or broken off, and inside are the snowy-white cloves of the pulp, sweet and with a very delicate but delicious flavour, unlike anything else I know of. But though dessert generally makes a finer display than any other part of dinner, it is not that to which most attention is directed. A cigar or a glass or two of sherry after the ladies are gone, and dinner is over.

"Many of the residences have billiard-rooms attached, in which case the usual custom is to retire there after dinner. Where no billiard-room is within reach, a chat in the verandah, a little meditation, or perhaps a book passes the hours pleasantly enough until bed-time. And as dinner is seldom over before eight o'clock, and the usual hour for rest is ten, it is not a very long interval between them that has to be disposed of.

"I think it is to be regretted that the people of Singapore so determinedly set their faces against every sort of entertainment which does not include a dinner. I am quite sure that much of the after-dinner time that is under the present system in a manner thrown away, might be more agreeably, and at the same time more profitably spent, if the custom were to set in that people should meet occasionally after dinner, and pass the evening in the same sort of social intercourse as is usual at home, and in most parts of the world.

"Such is the everyday life in Singapore."

Chinese Merchant Hosts Ball

   • A prominent Chinese merchant, Mr Kim Seng, hosted the first-ever ball for the European community in the mid-19th century to celebrate the completion of his warehouse, built from 1851-55. "The offices which occupy the upper floor of the godowns were the scene of the entertainment, the front room overlooking the river being fitted up as a dancing saloon," wrote Song Ong Siang in his book, *One Hundred Years' History of the Chinese in Singapore*. "At supper Mr Kin Seng's health was proposed by Mr Thomas Church in appropriate terms and drunk with the greatest enthusiasm by his guests. For the comfort of his native friends, some of the side rooms were laid out with tables of refreshments suited to their various tastes."

(preceiding page) Participants in Chingay procession.

A guest of the day described the event as follows: "Numerous invitations are issued to gentlemen and ladies of all tribes, who were requested to be present in their respective costumes on the appointed evening at the godown of Kim Seng. I had of course about me (as everybody else had) the usual prejudice of my own race, and therefore, on being presented to the master of the house, with his pig-tail, sharp features and Mongolian eyes, it was with much difficulty that I kept my mirth under polite restraint ...

"The ballroom was not much smaller than the body of a good-sized English church, with a row of pillars on each side, and under the galleries, behind which the spectators thronged ... The cluster of faces peering out from under the pillars was now and then lighted up with laughter as strangely united couples whirled past ...

A Schottische Scene

"A young lady from Calcutta, dressed after the most elaborate fashion of the city of palaces, got fearfully entangled in a schottische with a Chinese mandarin, whose large, jet-black tail descended considerably below his waist. As he hopped and frisked the tail flew about in the most dangerous manner. No doubt could be entertained, however, that the gentleman had been taking lessons for a fortnight or three weeks, because he really went through the business of the dance very respectfully. At length, as ill-luck would have it, one of his red slippers came off. A burst of laughter, which it was impossible to restrain, shook the fat sides of the host at this disaster, while the unhappy How Guim Foo quitted his partner and rushed, with his long tail like a comet, to regain his shoe – for to be shoeless is to be disgraced in Celestial eyes.

Tangled Tails

"At another time, and in another part of the room, the tails of two of the Chinese, as they passed one another back to back, hooked together, perhaps by the strings which tied them. While the gentlemen butted forward with their heads, after the manner of rams, to dissolve their involuntary partnership, the chosen partners ran into each other's arms and whirled on in the waltz without them.

"Becoming by degrees a little tired, I slipped behind the pillars for rest. Here I observed neat little tables in front of luxurious sofas, on which several Celestials reclined at their full length, smoking opium. They appeared to be in a delicious state of dreaminess, imagining themselves, perhaps, to be in the vicinity of the Lake of Lilies, with orange and tea trees blossoming around them. Near these were two or three Hindoos smoking the hookah; in the neighbourhood a solitary Turk who bore in his countenance an expression of infinite disdain for the infidels of all colours whom he saw around him ...

(overleaf) Downtown Singapore, silhouetted against the night sky.

A Chaos of Dainties

"To describe fitly the supper which followed, I ought to have studied for three years under some Parisian gastronome. It was a chaos of dainties, each more tempting than the other. All the fruits of the Indian Archipelago, of India, China and the West – some in their natural state, others exquisitely preserved – were piled around us. There were bird's-nest soups, puppy ragouts, pillaus of kangaroos' tails, fish of all kinds, and pastry in profusion. And then for the wines. All the wines that France, Germany and Hungary could produce sparkled on the board, and the most anxious care was taken that everyone should be supplied with what he most desired. While we were regaling ourselves, delicious strains of music, issuing from I know not where, stole into the apartment. This I thought much better than a noisy band, destroying or bewildering one's appetite, from a gallery immediately overhead."

Singapore's 35th Anniversary

Lt Colonel W.J. Butterworth, the Governor of the Straits Settlements between 1843-55, and his lady entertained the social elite of Singapore at a Ball in the Assembly Rooms to mark the 35th anniversary of the founding of Singapore. An account of that ball – held on the sixth of February 1854 – was reproduced in the book written by Donald and Joanna Moore. From this account we learn that "The Ball opened with a Quadrille, and was kept up with untiring energy. The polka, waltz, schottische and gallop followed in regular succession, accompanied by the most select music performed by the band of the 43rd M.N.I. and a private corps hired for the occasion. During the dances the scene was most enchanting – perhaps more fascinating to spectators than to those whose bright eyes, light hearts and nimble feet enjoyed the merry dance. Here, was seen a group of guests clad in the contrasted costumes of Europe and the Celestial empire; there, in close apposition, a dozen lords of the creation, displaying the flowing robes of Arabia and Persia – the magnificent and costly apparel of a Turkish Jew, the rose-vyeing garments of Siamese chieftains, the sparkling vesture of a Malay Prince, the uniforms of Consuls and of Native officers of the Anglo-Indian Army, whilst a gaily dressed Hebrew clothed in purple and fine linen, figures in the dance."

To illustrate further that Singapore, even then, was the melting pot of nationalities, the account described: "The walls of the room were covered with the flags of all nations visiting the port of Singapore, embracing the distinguishing standards of every people of the known world . . ."

Of course not all was waltzes and wine in the far-flung trading outpost of the British Empire. Singapore in those early days was beset by acts of piracy; crime and violence were rampant and riots erupted frequently. Today, the problem of lawlessness that made Singapore the Wild West of the East is part of her colorful past.

Recommended Reading

The understanding – and appreciation – of a country is often enhanced by background readings. A rewarding source of miscellaneous information concerning Old Singapore, with portraits and illustrations, is Charles B. Buckley's *An Anecdoctal History of Old Times in Singapore* (Singapore, Fraser and Neave, 1902). It covers the years 1819 to 1867, from the foundation of Singapore as a settlement under the East India Company until its transfer to the Colonial Office. Other books of this genre are Donald and Joanna Moore's *150 Years of Singapore History* (Singapore, Donald Moore Press Ltd, 1969), and Song Ong Siang's *One Hundred Years' History of the Chinese in Singapore* (Singapore, University Malaya Press, 1967). N.J. Ryan's *The Making of Modern Malaysia and Singapore* (Kuala Lumpur, 4th ed. rev. Oxford University Press, 1969) is meant as a textbook but provides for the general reader a historical background of the intertwining histories of Malaysia, Singapore, Sabah and Sarawak.

Several books have been written about Singapore's founder, Sir Thomas Stamford Raffles. Among them are the entertaining biography by Maurice Collis entitled simply *Raffles* (London, Faber and Faber, 1966); Nina Epton's *The Golden Sword*, being the dramatized story of Sir Stamford Raffles 1781-1826 (London, Oldbourne Press, 1957) which pays tribute to his good qualities, and the definitive biography by Charles E. Wurtzburg edited by Clifford Witting – *Raffles of the Eastern Isles* (Hodder and Stoughton, 1954).

For information on various facets of life in Singapore, there is Ronald McKie's *Singapore* (Sydney, Angus and Robertson, 1972), Leon Comber's *Chinese Temples in Singapore* (Singapore, Eastern Universities Press, 1958), Alan J. Elliott's *Chinese Spirit-Medium Cults in Singapore* (London, London School of Economics and Political Science, 1955), Marjorie Doggett's *Characters of Light*, a guide to the buildings of Singapore (Singapore, D. Moore, 1957), and Jean-Pierre Mialaret's *Hinduism in Singapore*, a guide to the Hindu temples of Singapore (Singapore, published for Asia Pacific Press by D. Moore, 1969).

The Singapore Government produces various publications such as *Singapore Facts and Pictures* 1982 (Information Division, Ministry of Culture), and the Singapore Tourist Promotion Board has a quarterly publication called *Singapore Travel* as well as pamphlets, all of which give up-to-date information about Singapore.

(overleaf) Lucky Plaza shopping centre on Orchard Road.

INFORMATION
SALE
Emperor

Appendix

Airlines

Aeroflot Soviet Airlines
100 Orchard Road #02-15
Tel: 2355252

Air France
400 Orchard Road #14-05
Tel: 7377166

Air Lanka
140 Cecil Street #02-00/B
PIL Building
Tel: 2236026

Air Mauritius
Furama Singapore Hotel
Tel: 5326262

Air New Zealand
Suite 1305 Ocean Building
Collyer Quay
Tel: 5358266

Air Niugini
101 Thomson Road
Tel: 2504868

Alitalia
140 Cecil Street #02-00/B
PIL Building
Tel: 2257233

Bimin Airlines of Bangladesh
Ground Floor, Alkaff Building
97 Market Street
Tel: 5352155

CAAC
51 Anson Road #01-53
Anson Centre
Tel: 2252177

Canadian Pacific Airlines
150 Cecil Street #10-05
Wing On Life Building
Tel: 2221977

Cathay Pacific Airways
#16-01 Ocean Buillding
Collyer Quay
Tel: 5331333

China Airlines
#04-01 Lucky Plaza
Orchard Road
Tel: 7372144

Czechoslovak Airlines
Suite 5, 3rd Floor
Holiday Inn
Scotts Road
Tel: 7379844

Garuda Indonesian Airways
#13-03 Goldhill Square
Tel: 2502888

Japan Airlines
#01-01 Hong Leong Building
Raffles Quay
Tel: 2210522

KLM-Royal Dutch Airlines
G2, Ground Floor
Mandarin Hotel Arcade
333 Orchard Road
Tel: 7377211

Lufthansa German Airlines
Ground Floor
Tanglin Shopping Centre
Tanglin Road
Tel: 7379222

Malaysian Airlines System
Singapore Shopping Centre
190 Clemenceau Avenue
Tel: 3366566

Pakistan International Airlines
#01-01 Ming Court Hotel
Tanglin Road
Tel: 7373233

Northwest Orient Airline
#03-29/30 Singapore Shopping Centre
Tel: 3367666

Philippine Airlines
#10-02/04
Park Lane Shopping Mall
Selegie Road
Tel: 3361611

Qantas Airways
Ground Floor, Mandarin Hotel
Orchard Road
Tel: 7373744

Royal Brunei Airlines
Royal Holiday Inn Shopping Centre
25 Scotts Road
Tel: 2354672

Sabena Belgian World Airlines
#01-31 International Plaza
Anson Road
Tel: 2217010

Scandinavian Airlines System
Ground Floor, Denmark House
Raffles Quay
Tel: 2251333

Singapore Airlines
SIA Building
77 Robinson Road
Tel: 2238888

Swissair
1st Floor, Lucky Plaza
Orchard Road
Tel: 7378133

Tarom Romanian Airlines
3 Coleman Street #03-01
Tel: 3381467

Thai Airways International
133 Cecil Street #08-01
Keck Seng Towers
Tel: 2242011

UTA French Airlines
400 Orchard Road #14-06
Orchard Towers
Tel: 7377166

Yogoslav Airlines
541 Orchard Road
#19-02/03 Liat Towers
Tel: 2353017

Clubs and Associations

Alliance Francaise
4 Draycott Park
Tel: 7378422

American Club
21 Scotts Road
Tel: 7373411

Apex Club of Singapore
Block 119 Bt Merah View #01-84
Tel: 2742306

Australian Association
Tanglin P.O. Box 426

Automobile Association of Singapore
336 River Valley Road
Tel: 7372444

Chinese Chamber of Commerce
47 Hill Street
Tel: 3378381

Deutsche Haus
12 First Avenue
Tel: 663156

Hollandsche Club
22 Camden Park
Tel: 4695211

Indian Chamber of Commerce
101 Cecil Street #23-01
Tel: 2222505

International Chamber of Commerce
4th Floor, Denmark House
Raffles Quay
Tel: 2241255

Japanese Association of Singapore
34 Scotts Road
Tel: 7373611

Japanese Chamber of Commerce
Unit 2304, CPF Building
Robinson Road
Tel: 2210541

Lions Club of Singapore
G.P.O. Box 438
Tel: 4400001

National Association of Travel Agents of Singapore
53-D Anson Centre
Tel: 2214588

New Zealand Association
Tanglin P.O. Box 426

Pacific Travel
c/o Singapore Tourist Promotion Board
Raffles City Tower
250 North Bridge Road #36-04
Tel: 3396622

Rotary Club of Singapore
Mandarin Hotel,
Orchard Road
Tel: 7372504

Singapore Hotel Association
24 Nassim Hill
Tel: 2359533

Singapore Jaycees
Unit 301, Midland House
112 Middle Road
Tel: 3374307

Singapore Manufacturers' Association
1st Floor, World Trade Centre
Telok Blangah Road
Tel: 2785211

Skal Club of Singapore
c/o Panan World Airways
Hong Leong Building
Tel: 94740

Swiss Club
36 Swiss Club Road
Tel: 4663233

Y Men's Club of Singapore
Metropolitan YMCA
70 Palmer Road
Tel: 2224666

YWCA
1 Orchard Road
Tel: 3373444

Foreign Missions

Arab Republic of Egypt (E)
75 Grange Road
Singapore 1024
Tel: 7371811

Argentina (CG)
302 Orchard Road #10-04
Tong Building
Singapore 0923
Tel: 2354231

Australia (HC)
25 Napier Road
Singapore 1025
Tel: 7379311

Bangladesh (CG) (TC)
101 Thomson Road #06-07
Goldhill Square
Singapore 1130
Tel: 2550075

Belgium (E)
10 Anson Road #09-24
International Plaza
Singapore 0207
Tel: 2207677

Brazil (E)
Orchard Road #15-03/04
Tong Building
Singapore 0922
Tel: 7343435

Britain (HC)
Tanglin Road
Singapore 1024
Tel: 4739333

Bulgaria (E, TR)
Scotts Road #09-09
Thong Teck Building
Singapore 0922
Tel: 7371111

Burma (E, TR)
15 St Martin's Drive
Singapore 1025
Tel: 2358763

Canada (HC)
8th Floor, Faber House
Orchard Road
Singapore 0923
Tel: 7371322

Chile (E)
16 Raffles Quay #43-03
Hong Leung Building
Singapore 0104
Tel: 2238577

Denmark (E)
101 Thomson Road #13-01/02
Goldhill Square
Singapore 1130
Tel: 2503383

Finland (E, TR)
101 Thomson Road #21-01/03
Goldhill Square
Singapore 1130
Tel: 2544042

France (E)
5 Gallop Road
Singapore 1025
Tel: 41664866

Germany, Federal Republic of (E)
Far East Shopping Centre
504 Orchard Road #14-00
Singapore 0923
Tel: 7371355

India (HC)
"India House"
31 Grange Road
Singapore 0923
Tel: 7376777

Indonesia (E)
"Wisma Indonesia"
7 Chatsworth Road
Singapore 1024
Tel: 7377422

Israel
Faber House
230 Orchard Road #11-230
Singapore 0923
Tel: 2350966

Italy (E)
Goldhill Square #27-02
101 Thomson Road
Singapore 1130
Tel: 2506022

Japan (E)
16 Nassim Road
Singapore 1025
Tel: 2358855

Korea, Democratic People's Republic of (E)
19 Fort Road
Singapore 1543
Tel: 3453044

Korea, Republic of (E)
Goldhill Square #10-01A/04,
101 Thomson Road, Singapore 1130
Tel: 2561183

Malaysia (HC)
301 Jervois Road
Singapore 1024
Tel: 2350111

Negara Brunei Darussalam (HC)
7-A Tanglin Hill
Singapore 1024
Tel: 4743393

Netherlands (E)
13-01/04, Liat Towers
541 Orchard Road
Tel: 7371155

New Zealand (HC, TC)
13 Nassim Road
Singapore 1025
Tel: 2359966

Norway (E)
16 Raffles Quay #17-01
Hong Leong Building
Singapore 0104
Tel: 2207122

Pakistan
20-A Nassim Road
Singapore 1025
Tel: 7376621

Panama (CG)
16 Raffles Quay #41-06
Hong Leong Building
Singapore 0104
Tel: 2218677

Philippines (E)
20 Nassim Road
Singapore 1025
Tel: 7373977

Poland (E)
100 Beach Road #24-11/12
Shaw Tower
Singapore 0718
Tel: 2942513

Rumania (E, TC)
41 Jalan Haram Setangkai
Singapore 1025
Tel: 4683424

Saudi Arabia (E)
10 Nassim Road
Singapore 1025
Tel: 7345878

Spain (C)
79 Robinson Road #27-00
CPF Building
Singapore 0106
Tel: 2204222

Sri Lanka (HC, TR)
51 Newton Road #1307-1312
Goldhill Plaza
Singapore 1130
Tel: 2544595

Sweden (E)
111 Somerset Road #05-08
Devonshire Wing
Singapore 0923
Tel: 7342771

Switzerland (E)
541 Orchard Road #17-03/04
Liat Towers
Singapore 0923
Tel: 7374666

Thailand (E)
370 Orchard Road
Singapore 0923
Tel: 2354175

United States of America (E)
30 Hill Street
Singapore 0617
Tel: 3380251

U.S.S.R. (E)
51 Nassim Road
Singapore 1025
Tel: 2351834

E-Embassy;
CG-Consulate General;
C-Consulate;
HC-High Commission;
TC-Trade Commission;
TR-Trade Representative

Hotels

SwB   : *Single with bath*
DwB   : *Double with bath*
++   : *plus 10% service charge; plus 3% govt tax*
CC   : *Honours credit cards*
D   : *Coffee shop, restaurant, bar or cocktail lounge*
E   : *Disco, nightclub*
S   : *Swimming pool*
*   : *Tennis, squash, badminton courts*
H   : *Sauna, massage, health club*
C*   : *Conference facilities for 200-500 persons*
C**   : *Conference facilities for more than 500 persons*
M   : *Meeting facilities for under 150 persons*

Deluxe

Dynasty
320 Orchard Road, Singapore 0923
Tel: 7349900
400 rooms.
SwB S$190-230; DwB S$220-250 ++
CC; D/E; S/H; C**

Mandarin Singapore
333 Orchard Road, Singapore 0923
Tel: 7374411
1,200 rooms.
SwB S$180-240; DwB S$215-275 ++
CC; D/E; S/H*; C**

Marco Polo
Tanglin Road, Singapore 1024
Tel: 4747141
603 rooms.
SwB S$180; DwB S$210 ++
CC; D/E; S/H; C*

Shangri-La
22 Orange Grove Road, Singapore 1025
Tel: 7373644
700 rooms.
SwB S$177-260; DwB S$212-295 ++
CC; D/E; S/H*; C**

International Chain Hotels

Century Park Sheraton
16 Nassim Hill, Singapore 1025
Tel: 7321222
464 rooms.
SwB S$175-200; DwB S$200-220 ++
CC; D/E; S/H; C*

Hilton International
581 Orchard Road, Singapore 0923
Tel: 7372233
435 rooms.
SwB S$140-210; DwB S$175-250 ++
CC; D/E; S/H; C**

Royal Holiday Inn
25 Scotts Road, Singapore 0922
Tel: 7377966
600 rooms.
SwB S$175-205; DwB S$205-255 ++
CC; D/E; S/H; M

Hyatt Regency Singapore
10/12 Scotts Road, Singapore 0922
Tel: 7331188
824 rooms.
SwB S$180-280; DwB S$210-310 ++
CC; D/E; S/H; C**

Oberoi Imperial
1 Jalan Rumbia, Singapore 0923
Tel: 7371666
600 rooms.
SwB S$150-170; DwB S$180-200 ++
CC; D/E; S/H; C*

Pavilion Inter-Continental
1 Cuscaden Road, Singapore 1024
Tel: 7338888
443 rooms.
SwB S$160-240; DwB S$200-280 ++
CC; D/E; S/H; C*

Singapore Forum
585 Orchard Road, Singapore 0923
Tel: 7371122
195 rooms.
SwB S$140-155; DwB S$160-175 ++
CC; D; S

Independent Hotels as good as chain hotels

Ming Court
Tanglin Road, Singapore 1024
Tel: 7371133
300 rooms.
SwB S$175-200; DwB S$200-225 ++
CC; D; S/H; C*

Orchard Hotel
442 Orchard Road, Singapore 0923
Tel: 7347766
350 rooms.
SwB S$170-185; DwB S$190-210 ++
CC; D; S; M

York
21 Mount Elizabeth, Singapore 0923
Tel: 7370511
400 rooms.
SwB S$175-200; DwB S$200-225 ++
CC; D; S/H*; M

Hotels with Old World Charm

Cockpit
6/7 Oxley Rise/Penang Road,
Singapore 0923
Tel: 7379111
182 rooms.
SwB S$120-160; DwB S$125-175 ++
CC; D; S; M

Goodwood Park
22 Scots Road, Singapore 0922
Tel: 7377411
262 rooms.
SwB S$205-235; DwB S$235-265 ++
CC; D/E; S*; CF

Raffles
1-3 Beach Road, Singapore 0718
Tel: 3378041
127 rooms.
SwB S$110-180; DwB S$130-200 ++
CC; D/E; S

Hotels for the Family

Garden
14 Balmoral Road, Singapore 1025
Tel: 2353344
86 rooms. (plus extension of 132)
SwB S$108; DwB S$128-200 ++
CC; D; S

Ladyhill
1 Ladyhill Road, Singapore 1025
174 rooms.
SwB S$125-165; DwB S$150-190 ++
CC; D; S; M

Lion City
15 Tanjong Katong Road, Singapore 1543
Tel: 7448111
162 rooms.
SwB S$72-80; DwB S$82-90 ++
CC; D; M

Metropole
41 Seah Street, Singapore 0718
Tel: 3363611
54 Rooms.
SwB S$90-95; DwB S$105-110 – +
CC; D

Negara
15 Claymore Drive, Singapore 0922
Tel: 7370811
104 rooms.
SwB S$80-125; DwB S$100-145 ++
CC; D/E; S

New Serangoon
305 Serangoon Road
Tel: 2937411
66 rooms.
SwB S$52; DwB S$69 – +
CC

Novotel Orchid Inn
214 Duneam Road, Singapore 1129
Tel: 2503322
321 rooms.
SwB S$108-138; DwB S$126-156 ++
CC; D; M

Queen's
24 Mount Elizabeth, Singapore 0922
Tel: 7376088
160 rooms.
SwB S$90; DwB S$100-110 ++

Seaview
Amber Close, Singapore 1543
Tel: 3452222
460 rooms.
SwB S$90-150; DwB S$110-150 ++
CC; D/E; S/H

Supreme
15 Kramat Road, Singapore 0922
Tel: 7378333
86 rooms.
SwB S$70; DwB S$80-120 ++
CC; D

Tanglin Court
Kim Yam/River Valley Road
Tel: 7373581
22 rooms.
SwB S$48-58; DwB S$58-68
D

VIP
5 Balmoral Crescent
Tel: 2354277
41 rooms.
SwB S$80-95; DwB S$94-104 +–
CC; D; S

Hotels offering Sun and Sea
(Ideal for casual holidays)

Apollo Sentosa
Sentosa Island
Tel: 4734388
162 rooms.
SwB S$140; DwB S$160 ++
CC; D; S*; C**

HUDC Holiday Chalets
110 East Coast Parkway
Tel: 4427135
169 rooms.
S$30-50 weekdays; S$36-70 weekends

Organizations with Hotel Accommodation
(Slightly different from the usual hotels, these are operated by non-profit making organisations)

Metropolitan YMCA
60 Stevens Road
Tel: 7377755
79 rooms.
SwB S$55; DwB S$60+5% s.c.
D; H*; M

Premier
Nassim Hill
Tel: 2355111
30 rooms.
SwB S$95.05; DwB S$113 +–
CC; D; S

RELC International House
30 Orange Grove Road
Tel: 7379044
128 rooms.
SwB S$85-95; DwB S$100-110
CC; D; C*

YMCA
70 Palmer Road
Tel: 2224666
50 rooms.
SwoB S$24; DwB S$38 + 5% s.c.
Temporary membership necessary
D; H*

No-Frills Hotels
(Small hotels offering basic facilities at low prices)

South East Asia
190 Waterloo Street, Singapore 0718
Tel: 3382394
51 rooms
SwB S$34; DwB S$41.20+3% s.c.
D

Victoria
87 Victoria Street
Tel: 3382381
47 rooms.
DwB S$58+3% tax
CC; D

Small Establishments
(Hotels with less than 50 rooms offering basic accommodation)

Chequers
418 Thomson Road
Tel: 2562266
28 rooms.
SwB S$60; DwB S$75 + –
D

Grand
25/26 Still Road South
Tel: 3455261
25 rooms.
DwB S$70
Use of communal kitchen, dining room for free.

Hotels with Good Shopping Arcades

Apollo Singapore
405 Havelock Road, Singapore 0316
Tel: 7332081
330 rooms.
SwB S$140; DwB S$160-180 ++
CC; D/E; C*

Merlin (renamed Plaza Hotel)
7500 Beach Road, Singapore 0719
Tel: 2980011
355 rooms.
SwB S$130-145; DwB S$150-170 ++
CC; D/E; S/H*; C*

Peninsula
3 Coleman Street, Singapore 0617
Tel: 3372200
315 rooms.
SwB S$125-130; DwB S$140-145 ++
CC; D/E; S/H; C*

Phoenix
Somerset Road, Singapore 0923
Tel: 7378666
300 rooms.
SwB S$132-154; DwB S$154-176 ++
CC; D; M

Good Quality Hotels
(Generally well furnished with extensive facilities)

Cairnhill
19 Cairnhill Circle, Singapore 0922
Tel: 7346622
200 rooms.
SwB S$120-155; DwB S$136-175 ++
CC; D; S/H; M

Equatorial
429 Bukit Timah Road, Singapore 1025
Tel: 7320431
224 rooms.
SwB S$130-220; DwB S$150-260 ++
CC; D/E; S; CF

King's
Havelock Road, Singapore 0316
Tel: 7330011
319 rooms.
SwB S$130-150; DwB S$150-170 ++
CC; D; M

Malaysia
40 Cuscaden Road
Tel: 7372911
220 rooms.
SwB S$125-145; DwB S$150-170 ++
CC; D; S; CF

Miramar
401 Havelock Road, Singapore 0316
Tel: 7330022
214 rooms.
SwB S$115-150; DwB S$135-170 ++
CC; D

President Merlin
181 Kitchener Road, Singapore 0820
Tel: 2950122
525 rooms.
SwB S$115-125; DwB S$125-140 ++
CC; D; C*

Royal
36 Newton Road, Singapore 1130
Tel: 2534411
321 rooms.
SwB S$95-115; DwB S$115-180 ++
CC; D; S/H; M

Tai-Pan Ramada
101 Victoria Street, Singapore 0718
Tel: 3360811
269 rooms.
SwB S$100-120; DwB S$115-135 ++
CC; D; H; M

Hotels for the Budget-Conscious Traveler
(These are comfortable with adequate facilities for most needs)

Air View
10 Peck Seah Street
Tel: 2211947
28 rooms.
SwoB S$21; DwoB S$28
D

Ambassador
42/46 Meyer Road
Tel: 4463311
170 rooms.
SwB S$80-120; DwB S$90-130 ++
CC; D/E/; S; M

Asia
37 Scotts Road, Singapore 0922
Tel: 7378388
146 rooms.
SwB S$105-125; DwB S$125-175 ++
CC; D; M

Ben
12 Bencoolen Street
Tel: 3360822
36 rooms.
SwB S$41; DwB S$49-51

Bencoolen
47 Bencoolen Street, Singapore 0718
Tel: 3360822
69 rooms.
SwB S$50-58; DwB S$60-68 ++
D

Broadway
195 Serangoon Road, Singapore 0812
Tel: 2924661
63 rooms.
SwB S$60-70; DwB S$70-80 – +

Grand Central
Cavenagh/Orchard Road, Singapore 0922
Tel: 7379944
365 rooms.
SwB S$120; DwB S$175 ++
CC; D/E; S/H; CF

Great Eastern
401 Macpherson Road, Singapore 1336
Tel: 2848244
151 rooms.
SwB S$85-95; DwB S$95-105
CC; D/E; H

Great Southern
36/42 A/B Eu Tong Sen Street
Tel: 93893
38 rooms
SwB S$26; DwB S$40-48 + –

Highway Inn
315 Clemenceau Avenue
Tel: 7375066
8 rooms.
SwB S$42; DwB S$46
D

Interlodge Ria Country Club
447/A Upper East Coast Road
Tel: 410222
40 rooms.
SwB S$60; DwB S$70 + –
CC; D/E; S*; M

Irama
435 Orchard Road
Tel: 7376333
28 rooms.
SwB S$47-57; DwB $61-72 + –
D/E

Kian Hua
81 Bencoolen Street
Tel: 3383492
19 rooms.
SwoB S$20; DwoB S$24-30

Lloyd House
2 Lloyd Road
19 rooms.
SwB S$45-70; DwB S$70-85+5% s.c.
D

Majestic
31/37 Bukit Pasoh Road
Tel: 2223377
24 rooms.
SwB S$34; DwB S$44
D

Mitre
145 Killiney Road
Tel: 7373811
19 rooms.
SwB S$20-25; DwB S$33-50
D; *

New Express Luen Kee
81-97 Middle Road
Tel: 3383477
35 rooms.
DwoB S$29-43

New Mayfair
40/44 Armenian Street
Tel: 3374542
27 rooms.
SwB S$47; DwB S$55+5% s.c.
CC; D

New Ritz
15 Bernam Street
Tel: 2219533
33 rooms.
SwB S$40; DwB S$48
CC; D/E

New Seventh Storey
228/229 Rochore Road
Tel: 3370251
38 rooms.
SwB S$54; DwB S$69
D

Pasir Ris
128 Elias Road
Tel: 5450918
29 rooms.
SwoB S$32; DwoB S$40+5% s.c.
CC; D

Savoy
10-A Upper Wilkie Road
Tel: 3376491
39 rooms.
SwB S$45; DwB S$50 + −
CC; D

Sloane Court
17 Balmoral Road
Tel: 2353311
34 rooms.
SwB S$70-80; DwB S$80-90 + −
D

South Seas
1 Mayo Street/5 Jalan Besar
Tel: 2944241
29 rooms.
SwoB S$40; DwoB S$50

Station
Railway Station, Keppel Road
Tel: 2221551
34 rooms.
SwB S$36; DwB S$45+5% s.c.
CC; D

Tiong Hoa
2/4/6 Prinsep Street
Tel: 3384522
15 rooms.
SwoB S$36; DwoB S$36-38

STPB Offices Worldwide

Head Office
Singapore Tourist Promotion Board
Raffles City Tower
250 North Bridge Road #36-04
Singapore 0617
Tel: 3396622
Telex: STBSIN RS 33375
Cable: TOURISPROM SINGAPORE

Regional Offices

Australia
8th Floor Goldfields House
1 Alfred Street, Circular Quay
Sydney, NSW 2000
Tel: 241-3771/2
Telex: STBSYD AA 27775
Cable: TOURISPROM SYDNEY

France
Centre d'Affaires Le Louvre
2 Place du Palais Royal
75044 Paris Cedex 01
Tel: 4297.16.16

Germany
6000 Frankfurt/Main, Friednesstr.5
Tel: (069) 231456/7
Telex: 4189742 STPF D
Cable: TOURISPROM FRANKFURT

Hong Kong
Singapore Tourist Promotion Board
Room 1402 Century Square
13 D'Aguilar Street
Central
Tel: 5-224052

Tokyo
Singapore Tourist Promotion Board
1st Floor, Yamato Seimei Building
1 Chome, 1-7 Uchisaiwai-cho
Chiyoda-ku, Tokyo 100, Japan
Tel: (03) 5933388
Telex: STBTYO J25591
Cable: TOURISPROM TOKYO

London
Singapore Tourist Promotion Board
1st Floor Carrington House
126-130 Regent Street
London W1R 5FE, United Kingdom
Tel: 01-4370033
Telex: STBLON G 893491
Cable: TOURISPROM LONDON

U.S.A.
Suite 1008, 342 Madison Avenue
New York N.Y. 10173
Tel: (212) 687-0385
Telex: 220843 SING UR
Cable: TOURISPROM NEW YORK

Los Angeles
Singapore Tourist Promotion Board
8484 Wilshire Boulevard
Suite 510, Beverly Hills
California 90211, USA
Tel: (213) 852 1901
Telex: 278141 SINGUR

Index